The

Year

of the

Poet X

November 2023

The Poetry Posse

inner child press, ltd.

The Poetry Posse 2023

Gail Weston Shazor
Shareef Abdur Rasheed
Teresa E. Gallion
hülya n. yılmaz
Kimberly Burnham
Tzemin Ition Tsai
Elizabeth Esguerra Castillo
Jackie Davis Allen
Joe Paire
Caroline 'Ceri' Nazareno
Ashok K. Bhargava
Alicja Maria Kuberska
Swapna Behera
Albert 'Infinite' Carrasco
Michelle Joan Barulich
Eliza Segiet
William S. Peters, Sr.

~ * ~

In order to maintain each poet's authentic voice, this volume has not undergone the scrutiny of editing. Please take time to indulge each contributor for their own creativity and aspirations to convey their uniqueness.

hülya n. yılmaz, Ph.D.
Director of Editing ~
Inner Child Press International

The Year of the Poet X
November 2023 Edition

The Poetry Posse

1ˢᵗ Edition : 2023

Publisher Information
1ˢᵗ Edition : Inner Child Press
intouch@innerchildpress.com
www.innerchildpress.com

ISBN-13 : 978-1-961498-11-2 (inner child press, ltd.)

$ 12.99

WHAT WOULD LIFE BE WITHOUT A LITTLE POETRY?

Dedication

This Book is dedicated to

Humanity, Peace & Poetry

the Power of the Pen

can effectuate change!

&

The Poetry Posse

past, present & future,

our Patrons and Readers &

the Spirit of our Everlasting Muse

In the darkness of my life
I heard the music
I danced . . .
and the Light appeared
and I dance

Janet P. Caldwell

Table of Contents

The Poetry Posse

Table of Contents . . . *continued*

Foreword
Children: Difference Makers

Jean-Michel Basquiat

Each month of 2023 a gifted, accomplished young person is featured in our monthly edition of The Year of the Poet. Our family of Poets 'The Poetry Posse 'dedicate a poem to that young person featured This month November, 2023 that young person is Jean-Michel Basquiat Born: 12/22/1960 Death: 08/22/1988 American artist born, raised in the Bronx, N.Y.C. Spoke 4 languages fluently, English, Spanish, French and Haitian Patwah.

Basquiat was a native of N.Y.C. His mother was from Puerto Rico, father Haiti. Young Jean evolved from Street art graffiti doing it on the streets of New York City. On buildings, other structures, subway trains, etc. His art evolved started to develop a unique style of using abstract images to tell a story, project a message dealing with institutional racism, police brutality particularly against young black Americans and Latino's. Corruption, oppressive government policies etc. It also included historical events that impacted on quality of life. He style was categorized as 'Neo-Expressionism' a liberal approach that uses techniques of many styles of art.

This included a generous use of colors, body parts, various structures, tools, shapes, forms that was consistent in conveying a message through his art. This was a departure of mainstream styles that consistently gave off a impression that it was meant to attract the elite thus to be embraced by the privileged. His departure from that was refreshing and soon started the public took notice including the well-known such as one Andy Warhol.

Jean often stayed on the lower East side of Manhattan bordering the East Village. That area was known to include artists of every genre. Poets, Musicians. Painters, you name it. It also was infested with heroine. Even the local park Tompkins Sq. Park was known as 'Needle Park 'Many artists were addicted. Many artists died.

Unfortunately, one such artist was Jean- Michel Basquiat. Please research more information about this gifted, special artist. Never underestimate what the youth can accomplish. Enjoy this enlightening edition of 'The year of the Poet'

Love and peace to y'all.
Yours truly

Shareef Abdur-Rasheed
Author, Poet, Activist

Preface

We, **Inner Child Press International, The Year of the Poet** and **The Poetry Posse** welcome you.

We are so excited as we are now offer unto you our eleventh month of our **10th** year of monthly publication of this enterprise, **The Year of the Poet**.

This particular year we have chosen to feature children who made/make a difference in enhancing the lives of all humanity. Read ~ Learn.

For those of you who are not familiar with our story, back in 2013, a few of us poets got together with the simple intention of producing a book a month. That was our challenge. Since that time the enterprise has blossomed and brought forth a fruit that seems to keep on growing as evidenced as we enter 2023.

Our purpose is simple. Through our lyrical words and verse, we not only wish to share our poetic works, but we also have the poetic naiveté to believe that we can assist in the growth of consciousness of the things that have an effect our collective humanity. Therefore, we welcome your readership. For more about what we are attempting to accomplish, have a look at our Publishing Web Site . . . www.innerchildpress.com. If you would like to know a bit more about this particular endeavor please stop by for a visit at :

Over the years, Inner Child Press has been socially active to bring awareness and catalog through literature the things that have an impact upon our world and its inhabitants. We have solicited, produced, underwritten and published quite a few volumes to that end. For more insight you may wish to visit : www.innerchildpress.com/the-anthology-market. If you are a writer, poet, or activist, you would be advised to keep a eye out for upcoming volumes should you desire to participate. All readers are welcomed as well. Note, that there is a myriad of published volumes that are available as a FREE PDF download as well as available for purchase at affordable prices.

We at this time extend to you our well wishes for your own personal journey and hope that you consider including us as a travel companion.

Bless Up

Bill

William S. Peters, Sr.

Publisher
Inner Child Press International
www.innerchildpress.com

Children
Difference Makers
Jean-Michel Basquiat
November 2023

by Kimberly Burnham, Ph.D.

"I don't listen to what art critics say. I don't know anybody who needs a critic to find out what art is."
~Jean-Michel Basquiat

Jean-Michel Basquiat (French: [ʒɑ̃ miʃɛl baskja]; December 22, 1960 – August 12, 1988) was an American artist who rose to success during the 1980s as part of the Neo-expressionism movement.

Basquiat first achieved fame as part of the graffiti duo SAMO, alongside Al Diaz, writing enigmatic epigrams in the cultural hotbed of Manhattan's Lower East Side during the late 1970s, where rap, punk, and street art coalesced into early hip-hop music culture. By the early 1980s, his paintings were being exhibited in galleries and museums internationally. At 21, Basquiat became the youngest artist to ever take part in *documenta* in Kassel. At 22, he was one of the youngest to exhibit at the Whitney Biennial in New York. The Whitney Museum of American Art held a retrospective of his artwork in 1992.

Basquiat's art focused on dichotomies such as wealth versus poverty, integration versus segregation, and inner versus outer experience. He appropriated poetry, drawing, and painting, and married text and image, abstraction, figuration, and historical information mixed with contemporary critique. He used social commentary in his paintings as a tool for introspection and for identifying with his experiences in the Black community, as well as attacks on power structures and systems of racism. His visual poetics were acutely political and direct in their criticism of colonialism and support for class struggle.

Since Basquiat's death at the age of 27 from a heroin overdose in 1988, his work has steadily increased in value. In 2017, *Untitled*, a 1982 painting depicting a black skull with red and yellow rivulets, sold for a record-breaking $110.5 million, becoming one of the most expensive paintings ever purchased.

Poets . . .
sowing seeds in the
Conscious Garden of Life,
that those who have yet to come
may enjoy the Flowers.

Poets, Writers . . . know that we are the enchanting magicians that nourishes the seeds of dreams and thoughts . . . it is our words that entice the hearts and minds of others to believe there is something grand about the possibilities that life has to offer and our words tease it forth into action . . . for you are the Poet, the Writer to whom the Gift of Words has been entrusted . . .

~ wsp

poetry is . . .

Poetry succeeds where instruction fails.

~ wsp

Now Available

Gail Weston Shazor

This is a creative promise ~ my pen will speak to and for the world. Enamored with letters and respectful of their power, I have been writing for most of my life. A mother, daughter, sister and grandmother I give what I have been given, greatfilledly.

Author of . . .

"An Overstanding of an Imperfect Love"
&
Notes from the Blue Roof

Lies My Grandfathers Told Me

available at Inner Child Press.

www.facebook.com/gailwestonshazor
www.innerchildpress.com/gail-weston-shazor
navypoet1@gmail.com

3

Slippin into darkness

And I was
Slipping into darkness
Slipping away
Slipping free
Free to see all the people
Slipping up the street
And around the corner
Standing with eyes open
Fixed on
Better places and better ways
To get it, make it, plan it
Their mind beyond the dreams
As I was
Slipping into darkness
I didn't know my name
Call me, find me, free me
In the slip, ready
Cash in my hand, money on my mind
And the drunken people
In the pews
Calling on the sword
To smite their unseen enemies
For the lack of mirrors
Turned from their own reflections
Less they see the need
Of corrected stance
When I heard my mother say
That I was slipping
Into darkness
Treading a edge
Between margins and marginalization
My brother sought my face
And yet, I didn't recognize
Me

Wholly, slowly, holy
No one understood
Save the man in the alley
How one gets lost
In broad daylight
Waiting to get found
Yet needing to be
Lost, remembered, alone
Sucking on my salvations
I sat on steps of promises
Though I know they are out of order
I've been
Slipping into darkness
On rhymes, on dreams, on grief
On counselor's wings
The program works
If you do it
Unless you can't remember how
I am
Slipping into darkness
The piper taunts, teases, tries
My patience
For what I think I need
And pretty soon
I'm gonna pay

100 steps

You chase my redemption
In a breathless hurry
Although I don't have many days
To number, i refuse to be rushed
Into the purility of nakedness
The vulnerability of a decision
That I am way too old to regret
And this does not mean
That I do not want you, contrary
I desire too much of you
For I would have the feast and famine
The lust and longing
Of one too long without any
Just to satisfy the sensation
And you I wait for
Bare headed in a hot sun
With sweat cooling the
White marble treads on either side
Of a busy street
Out here I push against time
For it is difficult to travel stones upwards
In hopes of finding a helping hand
I am lost to the son rising in the east
And the stinging rays causing tears
To fall from the corners of my eyes
My soul weeps here near the end of time
The lines marking my life run together
Until the continuity is palpable
From thumb to pinky
At the joining of wrists pressed tight
Against a longing for comfort
But yet I remain on the steps
Watching the traffic go by

On the occasion of a dry well

Take me to the edge of night
And release me into the void
In the lee of darkness
I am restless in the dawn
The light reveals much more
Than I wish to own
Insecurity and doubt
Ride my treads in evidence
The breath of faithlessness
Blows across my left shoulder
So I turn away
Though do not seek another path
On a trail I have oft renewed
When in mortal despair
Relegating the steps to memory
For I cannot seem to move
Beyond the familiar
Anointing on my dry skin
Of briars and weeds
As I pass the dangers imagined
Real and unreal
Nightmared in dreams
Though not in sleep
I am not afraid
For here the stars do not shine
And there is nothing
To be illumined
This is a lonely road
Nothing ahead and nothing beyond
Save the knowing of onlyness
Woven into a web of scars
Covering old wounds
So it is unexpected

The warmth of your hand
The tenderness in your voice
I stand still
And I remain indecisive
The next step remains untaken
For you never know when
An oasis bears no water
And every move toward it
Will only disappoint
As I have found many dry holes
But you continue to call my name
In tones of liquid azure
And I am so thirsty.

Alicja Maria Kuberska

Alicja Maria Kuberska – awarded Polish poetess, novelist, journalist, editor.

She is a member of the Polish Writers Associations in Warsaw, Poland and IWA Bogdani, Albania. She is also a member of directors' board of Soflay Literature Foundation, Our Poetry Archive (India) and Cultural Ambassador for Poland (Inner Child Press, USA)

Her poems have been published in numerous anthologies and magazines in : Poland, Czech Republic, Slovakia, Hungary,Ukraina, Belgium, Bulgaria, Albania, Spain, the UK, Italy, the USA, Canada, the UK, Argentina, Chile, Peru, Israel, Turkey, India, Uzbekistan, South Korea, Taiwan, China, Australia, South Africa, Zambia, Nigeria

She received two medals - the Nosside UNESCO Competition in Italy (2015) and European Academy of Science Arts and Letters in France (2017). Ahe also received a reward of international literary competition in Italy „ Tra le parole e 'elfinito" (2018). She was announced a poet of the 2017 year by Soflay Literature Foundation (2018).She also received : Bolesław Prus Prize Poland (2019), Culture Animator Poland (2019) and first prize Premio Internazionale di Poesia Poseidonia- Paestrum Italy (2019).

Street Singing
For Jean-Michel Basquiat

The street provides inspiration
- wealth and poverty side by side,
integration and segregation of pedestrians.
Colour everywhere - black and white

The artist intertwined poetry with painting
with quick brush strokes.
He generously added colourful abstraction
to the greyness of everyday life.
He incorporated social problems into graffiti
- opposition and rebellion on the walls
against injustice,
a call to fight for equal rights.

Memories of the painter faded.
The images still speak with the same voice
- they rap and sing in a hip-hop style

Symbol

You said – "I am a zero"
I thought – "I am a zero, too"
Does everyone have to be number one
in a race for wealth, power and fame?

Look
    – two connected zeros
form the infinity sign.
They contain within themselves
all numbers and the universe.

We carry
the memory of genes within us
and we are one of a kind.

Closed Door

The time of happy greetings passed.
Fate is playing with memories.

Nobody waits for me, nobody smiles.

I'm standing outside the door

Jackie
Davis
Allen

Jackie Davis Allen, otherwise known as Jacqueline D. Allen or Jackie Allen, grew up in the Cumberland Mountains of Appalachia. As the next eldest daughter of a coal miner father and a stay at home mother, she was the first in her family to attend and graduate from college. Her siblings, in their own right, are accomplished, though she is the only one, to date, that has discovered the gift of writing.

Graduating from Radford University, with a Bachelor's of Science degree in Early Education, she taught in both public and private schools. For over a decade she taught private art classes to children both in her home and at a local Art and Framing Shop where she also sold her original soft sculptured Victorian dolls and original christening gowns.

She resides in northern Virginia with her husband, taking much needed get-aways to their mountain home near the Blue Ridge Mountains, a place that evokes memories of days spent growing up in the Appalachian Mountains.

A lover of hats, she has worn many. Following marriage to her college sweetheart, and as wife, mother, grandmother, teacher, tutor, artist, writer, poet and crafter, she is a lover of art and antiques, surrounding herself, always, with books, seeking to learn more.

In 2015 she authored *Looking for Rainbows, Poetry, Prose and Art*, and in 2017, *Dark Side of the Moon*. Both books of mostly narrative poetry were published by Inner Child Press and were edited by hulya n. yilmaz in 2019, *No Illusions. Through the Looking Glass*, which was nominated to be considered for a Pulitzer Prize by the publisher and editor of Inner Child Press, ltd.

http://www.innerchildpress.com/jackie-davis-allen.php
jackiedavisallen.com

Remember His Name?

Beneath the umbrella of society's success,
He danced with gift of talent's fame,
Alas, he got swallowed up in its heady elixir.

And you ask, "Why did he not get help?"

He embraced the game of life, recklessly. He tossed
caution aside. He wanted more.
Something more. Something undefined, elusive.

What was it? Did he not have it all?

He struggled with discontentment:
With something unnamed? At a loss, alas,
He sank down into the well of darkest-despair.

Had he no other option?

He yielded to addiction's claim. He lost his life. He is no
more.
He is dead.

And I ask you, "What is his name?"

She Never Looked Back

In nothing did he find any pleasure.
Reaching out to no one,
No way to track his measure.

Abandoned, he had become undone,
Wondering what had gone wrong.

Inside the dimly lit bar, musicians
Soulfully played their instruments.
And the piano keys danced in tune,

While she, the jazzy one
With lips painted bright pink,

Glowered beneath the neon.
Suddenly she walked out the door!

Swiveling her hips,
Swishing her silky slips,
Unnoticed by one distracted.

And then, she walked down the street,
Never turning around to look back.

The night screamed and shrieked.
And eventually so did he;
As did his heart, which heavily fell.

Down to the subway stairs he ran,
Searching left and right.

Still under her beguiling spell,
He walked back up the street
Towards his flat, passing the noisy bar,

Dragging his weary feet, while she
Sought her freedom in a subway car.

Never had he felt so lost as he did
That night, of counting up the cost
Of climbing up the stars to the moon,

Where the blues were spinning, with him
holding nothing but a half empty glass.

Scattered on the floor,
Littering his forlorn room
Were bits and pieces of trash,

And, he waiting, dejected, all alone,
Except for depression's time-piece.

He threw himself across his bed,
Feeling as if he was sinking, about to drown.
For in nothing did he find any pleasure.

Isolated, he reached out to no one.
No way to track his measure.

Abandoned, he had become quite undone.
Questioning what had gone wrong,
He wondered if ever she would come back.

Or if in the writing, the error was
To be found in the second draft?

Lonely

He knew not what they thought;
He was but a young teen.
The room, the space, the air,
The same everywhere:

Silent as the grave
Whenever he appeared.
And still he sought,
Hoping, praying

To understand.
His heart heavy, longing,
Unsure, uncertain
What more it was that

He could do to prevent
Being ignored, ridiculed?
To help them comprehend
(They disinterested,

Self absorbed, unknowing, uncaring)
That all he wanted from them,
With every fiber of his being,
Was to be their friend.

But then, time
Like hope
Was running out
For him.

Tzemin Ition Tsai

Dr. Tzemin Ition Tsai comes from the Republic of China(Taiwan). In addition to being a professor of literature at a university, he is more committed to writing poems, novels, and proses. He is also an editor of "Reading, Writing and Teaching" academic text, an International editor of "Contemporary dialogues" literary periodical in Macedonia, and Vice-Chairman of the International Jury of the SAHITTO INTERNATIONAL AWARD in Bangladesh, and a columnist for "Chinese Language Monthly" in Taiwan.

In a wide range of literary creations, he is particularly fond of interesting stories or novels, and writing articles or poems about the feelings of nature and human beings. He has won many national literary awards. His literary works have been anthologized and published in books, journals, and newspapers in more than 55 countries and have been translated into more than 24 languages.

The Crystaline Sole

The cable car glides through the air like a bird
The scenery
A feast for the eyes
Transparent carriage
Crystal bottom
Floating on Sun-Moon Lake
Birds fly wildly in the warm breeze of a clear day
Beseeching the ape's call to cling to the window
Do not lose sight of the treetops
Sunset-kissed
Yilan Old Street
A narrow path winds its way to the base of the mountain
Each houses stand close together with chimney billowing
smoke
Small rustic inns
The fear of dusk when the streets are empty
The mountain cherry blossom falls in love with the Xishi
azalea
The sky-high rainbow is a dreamlike vision
The waves in my heart are
Like
The peaks that rise above the clouds
Will it be like a fleeting dream that is gone before we know
it?

Let Love Affairs Remain Unasked!

A lake of spring water
The dancing shadows of the waves
To stir
The sun is shining on the shore
The azalea tree's new green is so full of emotion that it is
uncontrollable
That throng of visitors
The voices continue to speak in a jumble
Like a newly awakened drunkard, is still in a state of flux
The light smoke and distant peaks are like two dancers in a
ballet
The water grass, swaying in the water
Not heed
The yachting world's slow drift away
A parting from what remains of that beach
If
Someone tries to pretend a transverse wave
A new word from the swallow's chirping
Love has already turned to water
Raised the cup, they are not allowing it to be half drunk
Am I to drink a hundred cups of the foam of the sea in
vain?
Who can forbid me to get drunk?

The Mountain Blossoms Speak To The Rushing Stream!

The Lake of the Sun and Moon
Still waters
Crystalline
A spoonful of early light
The silver trail of a carefree life behind me, on a clear day
The fine rain has finally ceased for a while
The wind
A leaf-like yacht, thought of as such
How much feeling can a tide convey?
I was a helpless bystander as...
To witness your presence in his travels
My Shadow and I
Crouched beneath the towering masts
The darkness
Perhaps I could turn the past into a flower in the pond?
Awash in
A well-filled pond
Alas
Only with one by one cherry blossoms and my thin sleeves
The shore-dwelling cuckoo, laughing to its heart's content
Can I shirk off my sadness with a little cheating?

Shareef
Abdur
Rasheed

Shareef Abdur-Rasheed, AKA Zakir Flo was born and raised in Brooklyn, New York. His education includes Brooklyn College, Suffolk County Community College and Makkah, Saudi Arabia. He is a Veteran of the Viet Nam era, where in 1969 he reverted to his now reverently embraced Islamic Faith. He is very active in the Islamic community and beyond with his teachings, activism and his humanity.

Shareef's spiritual expression comes through the persona of "Zakir Flo" . Zakir is Arabic for "To remind". Never silent, Shareef Abdur-Rasheed is always dropping science, love, consciousness and signs of the time in rhyme.

Shareef is the Patriarch of the Abdur-Rasheed Family with 9 Children (6 Sons and 3 Daughters) and 41 Grandchildren (24 Boys and 17 Girls).

For more information about Shareef, visit his personal FaceBook Page at :

https://www.facebook.com/shareef.abdurrasheed1
https://zakirflo.wordpress.com

very creative Jean Michel

told story through form's
Bits, pieces
Very creative Jean Michel
bits, pieces.
Very creative Jean Michel gave us puzzles to do.
Complex yet simple right
in front of your eyes.
Though you can't see it.
Whole array of senseless.
Nonsense is in our midst.
Jean Michel makes puzzles.
Can you solve them.
Body parts can you put the piece in the right spot
Where it fits.
Jean Michel a very creative artist forms, shapes, bits and
pieces.
Tell stories.
Don't ever under estimate what a young person can
do.
Scaq shouldn't had been one of
them.

She woke

in the early morn
reached over, he was gone
spot he laid still warm
thinking, what's going on?
about the warning from her
mom
something about him was wrong
couldn't put a finger on it but
the feeling was strong
might not be there from now on
got what he want and dashed
turned out not real wore a mask
tapped that a$$ and cash
shoulda listen to mama dear
she sees things load ' n ' clear
she tried to tell you,
you wouldn't hear
you knew her how many years?
wasn't mama always there?
and you met him five minutes ago
swore he was somebody you know
ain't it crazy how that $#!+ goes
phase's we all know too well
you try to impart truth to mind
some except it in due time
others with hard heads
ultimately got soft behinds
such is how lust induce blind trust
often in the worst among us
and you gave em props
build dem confidence up
then in time you find out
who you thought they was dem not.

Snatchin

fireflies out the sky in the warm summer night
hoping they will still glow glorious light
even though they were slowed when the snatcher
showed,
frightened?
now you know that's so
man just can't leave well enough alone
sooo..,
i wrote this little poem
talkin bout what we need from now on
preserve the beauty of the lands and seas
conserve the bounties of birds and bees
acknowledge creation's frailties,
the sanctity
right to be free from fright,
diminished rights
diminished quality of life
extinguish life's light
creates difficulty to see right, be right
survive through the night to greet the new day
say " hello sunrays "
reserve the energy to emerge free as a bird
flying around up, down from tree to tree
enjoying the scenery
bird, you sure be pretty
have you heard of mercy?
allows us to live, free.
Free? Free? Free?
is freedom really an actuality?
or the dream it will be eventually
realm of serenity
the time our eyes are still open and still can see
before they're closed permanently.

something to be said about duty to the things of beauty
responsibility is constructive continuity
as opposed to destructive, indifferent inconsistency
yo brother man, sister women preach to me
let me hear you say..,
(((UNIVERSAL HARMONY

Kimberly Burnham

A brain health expert with a PhD in Integrative Medicine, Kimberly Burnham has lived in tropical Colombia; in Belgium during the Vietnam War; in Japan teaching businessmen English; in diverse international Toronto, Canada; and several places in the US. Now, she's in Spokane, WA with her wife, Elizabeth, two sets of twins (age 11 & 14) and three dogs. Her recent book, *Awakenings: Peace Dictionary, Language and the Mind, a Daily Brain Health Program* includes the word for peace in hundreds of languages. Her poetry weaves through 80+ volumes of *The Year of the Poet, Inspired by Gandhi, Women Building the World*, and *A Woman's Place in the Dictionary*. She is currently working on several ekphrastic writing projects. One is a novel, *Art Thief Cracks Healing Code for Parkinson's Disease* and the other is non-fiction, *Using Ekphrastic Fiction Writing and Poetry to Create Interest and Promote Artists, Writers, and Poets*.

http://www.NerveWhisperer.Solutions

https://healthy-brain.medium.com/bears-at-the-window-of-climate-change-d1fb403eeaf3

Only The Good

Only the good die young
a song's refrain dances inside my head
as I read the bio of an artist
Jean-Michel Basquiat, a musician
success by 22 dead by 27
art and music creative

Is it true
the young and the good
the bad and the old die
one has more time to create share and grow
one's time is snatched away

Perhaps it is not so much time
as what we pack in that matters
says an old person
the young expecting so much more time
as if each is entitled to a certain amount
and we are
but there is no certainty
no clear entitlement
only today
and for sure
only this moment to be good or bad

A Prayer Spread Over Us

talk communicate believe

cousins pray for peace

salaam shalom silim sulh

The Lines and Energy of Peace

Shanti in 18 forms
unfamiliar curves and lines
reaches out, a sound brought forth
a pen tracing chard fire on white
bringing to life an idea
a dream of hope,
conjuring actions and energy

Shanti in 18 words
संधि , শান্ছি, 'Sãdʰi
শান্তি, ಶಂಠೆ, თანხ૦
Шанти, شانت, ಜುಂ
शांति, śānti, નિરાંત

ಶಂಠೆ, ൧ ≺, [ᵀᴹ
شانتى, सांटी, ႜ૭ৡᲘᄝ

Elizabeth E. Castillo

Elizabeth Esguerra Castillo is a multi-awarded and an Internationally-Published Contemporary Author/Poet and a Professional Writer / Creative Writer / Feature Writer / Journalist / Travel Writer from the Philippines. She has 2 published books, "Seasons of Emotions" (UK) and "Inner Reflections of the Muse", (USA). Elizabeth is also a co-author to more than 60 international anthologies in the USA, Canada, UK, Romania, India. She is a Contributing Editor of Inner Child Magazine, USA and an Advisory Board Member of Reflection Magazine, an international literary magazine. She is a member of the American Authors Association (AAA) and PEN International.

Web links:

Facebook Fan Page

https://free.facebook.com/ElizabethEsguerraCastillo

Google Plus

https://plus.google.com/u/0/+ElizabethCastillo

Electrifying Art

Fearless, creative and driven
Basquiat, a cultural icon,
A Neo-Expressionist
Highly expressionistic masterpieces
An artist ahead of his time.
His angst depicted in his works,
Coined as the American Street Art Pioneer
He once said "The more I paint, the more I like everything."
Basquiat and his crown,
A King of his own.

Indigo Child

i am not of this world -
i came from an abysmal chaos-
but from this beautiful chaos, Desiderata was born-
a child of the Universe, precious and golden
a lovely old soul beyond time and space-
often misunderstood by mediocre minds-
but applauded by great free thinkers -
i long for a world enveloped in serenity-
inhabited by empaths with great sensitivity
a loner I may be but this is who I am-
but i've got this deep connection with things around me
an indigo girl at birth-
my temporary sanctuary is the Earth
lone wolves gather at my feet-
for i am their Goddess in human form.

Awakenings

A cast-away soul in his solitary moment,
Floating into a never-ending circle of uncertainty
In denial of all things hitting him in the eye
Or could it be that he just can't dare to face dire reality?
A deep-seated fear sets in rooted from the world's cruelty.
Shielding himself from dark forces,
But wake-up calls are beyond his control
He wants to awaken from this abstract dream
Mysterious vibrations preventing him to even scream
Delusions overwhelming him in every heart beat.
A spectrum of enveloped ideas only his mind can conceive,
Out of this swirling darkness he awakened from being
naïve
Bid adieu to his grueling nightmare
Awaiting for the dawning of a new day
To see the light welcoming him again.

Joe
Paire

Joseph L Paire' aka Joe DaVerbal Minddancer . . .
is a quiet man, born in a time where civil liberties
were a walk on thin ice. He's been a victim of his
own shyness often sidelined in his own quest for
love. He became the observer, charting life's path.
Taking note of the why, people do what they do. His
writings oft times strike a cord with the
dormant strings of the reader. His pen the rosined
bow drawn across the mind. He comes full-frontal
or in the subtlest way, always expressing in a way
that stimulate the senses.

www.facebook.com/joe.minddancer

Links Of A Chain

What interpretation of anything binds us together
Jean-Michel Basquait, young and influential
An artist with credentials,
few can speak on what he's been through
yet the song remains the same

I wanted to be him, before he was believed in
An artists brush for me is just like an ink pen,
Or a link-pin, who knows or who shows
How close we're truly linked in
His life, my future,
Are still based on the times of Lincoln

Have you thought about making a difference,
Referencing the artistry of one so different
A labyrinth of collaborations, connected in time
Ofttimes my creations are collected in mind
This time, these times are unlike any other
I salute Jean-Micheal Basquiat aka SAMO
From graffiti on walls, to museum halls

When you see them fall, tighten up your reins
Life is art, and the song remains the same

Blocked Scenes

My view has been obscured by life circumstance
My demeanor will change,
depending on where I stand
I miss the sunset captured in apertures
I miss my souls rest, I'm not sure if I'm happy here

New birds, new trees, and a host of new creatures
I film what I see, but my Sunscape's a feature
The longitude and latitude of life has changed
My east and western view is not the same
The night sky holds the night eyes,
I've had an issue with my third eye

The flora needs time to rise from winter
The weeds seem to find a way to enter
Take my camera and return to sender
If I lose my muse, I may take a bender
This lack of a sunset is a total surrender
But I rise to blue skies and the clouds remember

There's a branch in the middle of my canvas
Like some happy accident from a curly fro.
This new type of scenery I barely know
I can't wait for spring when the flowers show

There is more to the orbit of orbs and shadows
I'll seek moments rather than time my dreams
I'll absorb a new energy, to free blocked scenes

So Close To His Story

So close to where some believe it all began
Some wars never end, and start over again
New generations with a new taste for hate
The truth needs proof, but a lie seems okay
The world is full of popularity seekers
Stop it with the profits, fact check the leaders

Fat checks aren't leaders, yet everything costs
A poor man with a policy, is a preordained loss
Is philanthropy a lost art, or naturally a lost cause
No one wants to help anyone
without some sort of clause
a reason to deceive in the fine print of contracts
tis the season believe in,
how to get your money back

I long for a new view of life
Who will change my opinion
Some words are etched in stone
In a time, I wasn't living in
Delivering the proper message
Is a massive undertaking
What divinity wouldn't offend me
Whose rule do you pray to.
Choose wisely, or realize
Find the one where you can stay true
Horseshoes and no cigars
You are not the father!
The closer we think we are
We seem to go a little further

hülya
n.
yılmaz

Professor Emerita, hülya n. yılmaz is a published author, literary translator, and Co-Chair and Director of Editing Services at Inner Child Press International. Her poetic work appeared in numerous anthologies of global endeavors and was presented at various literary events in the U.S. and abroad. In 2018, WIN honored yılmaz with an award of excellence. Since 2017, her two poems remain permanently installed in *Telepoem Booth* – a U.S.-wide poetic art exhibition. hülya finds it vital for everyone to seek a deeper sense of self, and writes creatively to attain a comprehensive awareness for and development of our humanity.

hülya n. yılmaz, a traveler on the journey called "life" . . .

Writing Web Site
https://hulyanyilmaz.com/

Editing Web Site
https://hulyasfreelancing.com

Marginalized Even in Death

Found dead in his residence
at the age of 27.

"Heroin overdose",
concluded the media asap,
though the cause of death
was not yet determined at the time.

When Black, you just must be
either a thug or a drug addict.
Even your lifeless body
undergoes the scrutiny
of racism's claws.

Headlines mostly omitted
what an exceptional talent he was,
that the images in his works
unraveled the intentional oversights
of his-story, how successfully he was able
to see through the lens of slavery and of the
relentless colonizers of authentic cultures.

"Jean-Michel Basquiat.
Dead at 27.
Possible overdose."

Lenses

A monolithic worldview

has been passe for centuries,

though the news does not seem

to have reached the doorsteps

of modern-day Neanderthals as of yet.

Clean your lenses, if you can.
If not, drop them now in the garbage can.

The Art of Overt Painting

images and text

art history and racism

slavery, classism

Teresa E. Gallion

Teresa E. Gallion was born in Shreveport, Louisiana and moved to Illinois at the age of 15. She completed her undergraduate training at the University of Illinois Chicago and received her master's degree in Psychology from Bowling Green State University in Ohio. She retired from New Mexico state government in 2012.

She moved to New Mexico in 1987. While writing sporadically for many years, in 1998 she started reading her work in the local Albuquerque poetry community. She has been a featured reader at local coffee houses, bookstores, art galleries, museums, libraries, Outpost Performance Space, the Route 66 Festival in 2001 and the State of Oklahoma's Poetry Festival in Cheyenne, Oklahoma in 2004. She occasionally hosts an open mic.

Teresa's work is published in numerous Journals and anthologies. She has two CDs: *On the Wings of the Wind* and *Poems from Chasing Light*. She has published three books: *Walking Sacred Ground, Contemplation in the High Desert* and *Chasing Light*.

Chasing Light was a finalist in the 2013 New Mexico/Arizona Book Awards.

The surreal high desert landscape and her personal spiritual journey influence the writing of this Albuquerque poet. When she is not writing, she is committed to hiking the enchanted landscapes of New Mexico. You may preview her work at

http://bit.ly/1aIVPNq or *http://bit.ly/13IMLGh*

Tragic Genius

A young man living in the hood
in a Manhattan neighborhood
is Destined for greatness
in expressions in the arts.

At 27 already broken by the gangsta heroin.
The tragic death of a genius
left relics of artistic expression
that thrives in the 21st century.

Open your arms to receive the legacy
of a broken Prince left to the ages.

Today Mama

It is in the light of morning,
I rise in gratitude you were here
and loved me dearly.

Today the weight of your leave
drowns me in the river of grief.
I awaken still knowing deep inside
you are always with me.

I know you are okay.
Human attachment weighs me down.
You ride with me in the heavenly planes.

Our Spiritual guides lead us
to the river of light.
Love shines with brilliance
and we smile holding hands.

We have unfinished business
that requires another meeting
on the physical plane.

I smile, wandering who will be
mother, father, sister or brother
next time we meet.
You smile and fade into the light.

I Want to Shake You

I want to shake you until
all the wax runs out of your ears.
May you hear songs of love
for the first time.

I want to shake you until
your nine holes of jade
release the negative elixir
binding you to earth.

I want to shake you until
you scream I forgive myself
and every person I gave a negative kiss.
Then watch you move forward
on your journey.

I want to shake you until
you surrender
all your negative baggage
and dance in the light.

I want to shake you until
the blender is streaming light
like a holy lantern
to radiate your pathway.

Come near to me.
I want to shake you until.

Ashok K. Bhargava

ASHOK BHARGAVA is a poet, writer, inspirational speaker and a literary consultant. He has attended poetry conferences in Italy, Turkey, India and Philippines. His latest book "Riding the Tide" about his battle with cancer has been translated and published in Arabic, Hindi, Telugu and Bengali languages. He is a contributing writer to several anthologies worldwide including World Poetry Almanac 2014. He has been published in numerous print and online magazines.

Ashok has won many accolades including Poet Ambassador to Japan, Kalidasa International award, World Poetry Lifetime Achievement award, Writers Beyond Borders Peace award and Tapsilog Leadership award for his community involvement. He is founder of Writers International Network Canada Society to discover, nourish, recognize and celebrate writers, poets and artists and to assist them to network with the community at large. He is the author of eight books of poetry and one anthology. He is Artist-in-Residence at Moberly Arts & Cultural Centre and also co-edits the literary section of The Link Newspaper.

Eccentric Dichotomies

For Jean-Michel Basquiat

Dreams of delights
Sink into sadness
Promises of pleasures
Descend into decay.

The ugly
Reality of addiction
Plays out contradiction of
The ephemeral permanence.

A heroin overdose spin
The physical and spiritual existence
Outwards to the other side
Of the rainbow.

A perpetual continuity
Creating a universe of its own
Not of sorrow
But of grace.

You Left Me Behind

As I try to stop you to talk to me
You drive away
Furiously
Calling police
Demonizing me

I had come
To make peace with you
You said
You aren't talking to me

I see the empty street
Smiling at me

I look around
Confused.

Unbridled

Agony keeps me awake
with anxiety upon anxiety
returning with
unheard loss like mine.

My mind keeps replaying
that last conversation
in the townhouse
her index finger pointed at me.

What's the difference
between careless and churlish?
I'm not sure
I want to know.

With every new breath
with each beat of my heart
I regret the moment
I lost you.

Caroline
'Ceri Naz'
Nazareno
Gabis

Caroline 'Ceri' Nazareno-Gabis

Caroline 'Ceri Naz' Nazareno-Gabis, author of Velvet Passions of Calibrated Quarks, World Poetry Canada International Director to Philippines is a multi-awarded poet, editor, journalist, educator, peace and women's advocate. She believes that learning other's language and culture is a doorway to wisdom.

Among her poetic belts include **Gabrielle Galloni Memorial Panorama International Youth Award 2022**, Panorama Youth Literary Awards 2020, 7th Prize Winner in the 19th, 20th and 21st Italian Award of Literary Festival; Writers International Network-Canada ''Amazing Poet 2015'', The Frang Bardhi Literary Prize 2014 (Albania), Poet Journalist Award 2014 (Tuzla, Istanbul, Turkey) and World Poetry Empowered Poet 2013 (Vancouver, Canada). She's a featured member of Association of Women's Rights and Development (AWID), The Poetry Posse, Galaktika Poetike, Asia Pacific Writers and Translators (APWT), Axlepino and Anacbanua. Her poetry and children's stories have been featured in different anthologies and magazines worldwide.

Links to her works:

http://panitikan.ph/2018/03/30/caroline-nazareno-gabis/

https://apwriters.org/author/ceri_naz/

http://www.aveviajera.org/nacionesunidasdelasletras/id1181.html

Epigrams

Basquiat married the art and letters,

He dismantled dichotomies

of the society,

If he is alive today,

He'll pull your hair

To give you whimsical street art,

His raps, hip-hop, and punks,

made galleries of enlightenment

and revelations of cultural victories.

I left my heart

I left my heart
like a box of tissue paper,
at the front mirror of your room,
a piece of it in my palm,
close to my chest,
wherever i go,
it sticks to my face,
it wipes the tears,
whenever i think of you,
from a long and winding road,
it covers my nose
to get rid of the dust
that makes me sneeze
and gives me rolling wet diamonds,
again, and again,
because my home is you.

Heaven's Medley

i set my eyes on you,
your glimpses are rainbows
shaped in rhymes,
embroidered with riddles
of vibrant hues,
like youthful years
full of sunny and rainy days in medley
the jubilation of stars in heavens
so distant, but twinkling
and penetrating my heart,
even the night is a doom,
with lonesome movies
out of the blue.

Swapna Behera

Swapna Behera is a trilingual poet, translator, environmentalist, editor from India and author of seven books of different genres including one on children's literature on Environment. She is the recipient of International UGADI AWARD 2019, honoured from Gujurat Sahitya Akademi 2022, 2021 International Poesis Award of Honor as Jury, Pentasi B World Fellow Poet, Honoured Poet of India from Seychelles Government and International awards from Algeria, Morocco, Kajhakhstan, modern Arabic Literary Renaissance of Egypt, International Arts Council Argentina etc. Her stories, poems, articles are published in many International and National magazines and ezines. Her poem A NIGHT IN THE REFUGEE CAMP is translated into 67 languages. She has received over 60 National and International Awards. At present she is the Cultural Ambassador for India and South Asia of Inner Child and the life member of Odisha Environmental Society

Email
swapna.behera@gmail.com

Web Site
http://swapnabehera.in/

Jean – Michel Basquiat

the pioneer
of Neo expressionism movement
paintings as a tool to introspect
social commentary is his slogan
Dichotomies versus poverty
Integration versus segregation
Inner versus outer experience in life
poetry, drawing and painting
text and image
abstract figuration mingled
with historical information
his visual poetries are political
against colonialism;
support for class struggle
his painting untitled depicts a skull
with red and yellow rivulets
sold in a record price
enigmatic epigrams all over primitivism
accidental overdose of drug killed Jean Basquiat
fearless and a cultural icon
reflects raw talent
whose graffiti art resonates
against racism
he is not a person but a legend
whose voice via graffiti art
resonates against racism
can a legacy ever die?

micro plastics: the ultimate killers

just listen to the baby
here or there someone cries
microplastics in the breast milk
the baby suffocates now in the ventilator
microplastics, the killers are
in the heart tissues
in food, air, water and soil
the toxic substance
in the environment
in the placental tissues
in human blood
the great killer is invisible
contaminating our oceans
kills wild life in the forests
we forget the plastics after using them
but they leave terrible footprints
are we all blind or deaf?
they are the tiniest debris in sea weeds
or between my toes
we make the waste that nature can never digest
no more addiction for plastics
it starts from the land and spoils five elements
ecofriendly food packaging is the clarion call
let there be plastic free cosmetics
there are more microplastics in the sea
than stars in the milky way
stop the catastrophe, stop the killer

when the diaspora bleeds

the spectrum spreads
in the anvil
ask the temples, mosques or war fields
the diaspora bleeds
in the full moon
or at dark nights
the artisans deleted the tears
of their desires for their wives, children
the young soldier cries for a home-made roti
it is a challenge always
the animals are carried to the slaughtering house
their calves, partners left behind
who doesn't want a grave in his own soil?
empowerment is at stake in the tectonic movement
a child's diaspora heart runs after the butterflies
alphabets to eyes; the sojourn journey begins
our so-called Gods reach the Earth
with their ethical scriptures
are they happy now?
the soul flies somewhere
ultimately the sporadic galaxy splits
yes, somewhere or the other
the diaspora dot moves like virgin dew drops

Albert
'Infinite'
Carrasco

Albert "Infinite The Poet" Carrasco is an urban poet, mentor and public speaker.

Albert believes his experience of growing up in poverty, dealing with drugs and witnessing murder over and over were lessons learnt, in order to gain knowledge to teach. Albert's harsh reality and honesty is a powerfully packed punch delivered through rhyme. Infinite grew up in the east part of the Bronx and still resides there, so he knows many young men will follow the same dark path he followed looking for change. The life of crime should never be an option to being poor but it is, very often.

Infinite poetry @lulu.com

Alcarrasco2 on YouTube

Infinite the poet on reverbnation

Infinite Poetry

http://www.lulu.com/us/en/shop/al-infinite-carrasco/infinite-poetry/paperback/product-21040240.html

Jean-Michel Basquiat

You can see my tags and pieces as my markers and spray paint leave art on new york walls as a graff canvas. it wasn't just walls, you'll see my name SAMO on new york buses and trains. I'm just a young visionary sharing my talent or my art loving community and I do so, so... uniquely.. It all started when i was a kid growing up in brooklyn drawing and writing about poverty and racism as an expression. my mother was the one that urged me to pursue my passion, i listened and created a lane of my own, there was no comparison. my art was giving vision of my thoughts without verbal manifestation. I made it, I mean I became a household name for art without borders or frames. i went through a lot, my parents divorced, my mother lost her sanity and my father was abusive, dealing with the two situations is how i learned what abuse is. Pain and success mixed with a lot of partying and the use of heroin is how I gained a deadly addiction that would kill me when I was only twenty seven. My name is Jean-Michel Basquiat, my Neo-Expressionism, 1982 painting of a skull, sold for $110.5 million at a Sotheby's auction..

Skipping rocks

I used to love to skip rocks.. Splash splash splash.. While skipping rocks I was told my dad passed so now I pass on skipping rocks.. Tears tears tears. Now. I stare at the water to see if i see reflections of my father, when I'm the one it's reflecting.

I let it grace my toes as it cleanses my soul, it's like if I'm going through baptism Every time I step in wisdom and think of him.

My daddy my pops my maker... I only knew for twelve shorts years.. Tears tears... In six years I'll be 12 years older than him when he disappeared.. Tears tears, my son is 12 the same age that i was when he disappeared, tears tears. For him, I'm doing everything in my power to remain here.

I don't need him to be worrying about his pops while he skips rocks. so i put down the pyrex and stopped the cooking of rocks. When I leave him it's going be my calling, not early in life like my daddy, like the hospital calling mommy, like mommy coming to get me, while I looked at rocks hydroplaning, up and down, defying gravity then stop.... like the heart rate monitor on my father. Like I said I no longer skip rocks... No need, my heart beat skips as I think of my pops.

Headless Horsemen

I now levitate through the apocalyptic region as a reaper due to loosing my stallion while battling in the underworlds dominion, he was stuck in the heart with a speared pole, as I leaned over and decapitated my foe, he now rest as a caucus on the battle field of the lost, I vowed to hover forever in the realm of the infinite, the sun doesn't shine but the moon still glows amongst the shadows of freelance souls, it renders negative reflections. I hear yells and screams from down yonder on the eternal path of skeleton paved roads, as I get nearer the sounds become clearer, I see dark reapers awaiting at Armageddons gate for for new souls to appear, you hear the clinging of swords in celebration, I swing my sword with arbitration 1 2 3 4 negative reapers are now headless horsemen, now the souls of the lost kids that was screaming and yelling won't get stolen like mines was, I choose to stay in limbo, in the realm of the infinite, so my dying breeds souls rise up as spirits

Michelle Joan Barulich

Michelle Joan Barulich

Michelle Joan Barulich was born in Honolulu, Hawaii on the island of Oahu. She started writing poetry and songs with her younger brother Paul. They have written many songs in their teen years. She is currently studying Alternative Medicine and would like to become a Homeopathic Doctor. Michelle loves all kinds of animals and birds; she does wild rehabilitation. She has also rescued rock pigeons that make great pets.

https://www.facebook.com/michelle.barulich

Graffiti to Glory

Jean-Michel what a talented artist

You did things your way with a twist

His unique style made people think

From poverty to riches

You made an impact

From New York city and abroad

Your art, style, and notoriety

will live on...

In this City

Those city days have passed away
Those city nights have suspended me
Your city lights find a way to get to me
You hand out all the pleasures
But along with it comes the pain
I don't want to be a wash out in this city
You tempted me with all the colors
And all your lights around me
I'm not the first to fall
Everyone wants to be a somebody
In this city
I don't know why it is.
Getting myself in these predicaments
Just want to be me, just me.
They say your worth what you owe out
I don't want my dream to burn out
I don't want to burn out too fast
Hear the boys sing
Those city nights have called my name
Those city days have spoken to me
There is no rule to art
It's whatever you got
Your city nights
Make me feel cool
Your city days
Makes me feel warm
It gives you fame
But how do you play the game?
Dressed in black, it makes me how I want to feel
Your city ways give me hope
Your city pays the deeds
Makes me lose my mind

I'm hoping to win as the coin turns
In this city
Hear the boys say
Hey, hey in this city!

His Love

As he lays out his plan
His mind is drenched with vivid colors and shades
Hoping to capture what he sees on canvas
Each movement with brush he seeks for perfection
May it be a sunset, an ocean wave, or a child's face
He paints gladly, he struggles to make it right
Hoping to stumble across the light
Every glide of the brush he makes his heart beats faster
He knows he must keep his hands from shaking, every muscle aches
But this is what he loves best
His finished project he now holds in his weary hands
He gives his untold story
Behind the picture painting he smiles back at you.

Eliza Segiet

Eliza Segiet graduated with a Master's Degree in Philosophy at Jagiellonian University.
Received *Global Literature Guardian Award* – from Motivational Strips, World Nations

Writers' Union and Union Hispanomundial De Escritores (UHE) 2018.

Nominated for the Pushcart Prize 2019, 2021.

Laureate *Naji Naaman Literary Prize 2020, International Award Paragon of Hope* (2020),

World Award 2020 *Cesar Vallejo* for Literary Excellence.

Laureate of the Special Jury *Sahitto International Award* 2021, World Award *Premiul Fănuş Neagu* 2021.

Finalist *Golden Aster Book* World Literary Prize 2020, *Mili Dueli* 2022, Voci nel deserto 2022.

At the international Festival of Poetry CAMPIONATO MONDIALE DI POESIA (2021/2022) she won the title of vice-champion of the world.

Award BHARAT RATNA RABINDRANATH TAGORE INTERNATIONAL AWARD (2022).

Erudite of Understatements
In memory of Jean-Michel Basquiat

Unsaid signs
still say more
than a defined dash, dot
or any other shape.

Between the birth and death
he made the world aware
that a spray painting on the wall
or brush strokes on anything -
will last longer than a human breath.

Appreciated when he was among the living,
unforgotten after passing
through the narcotic, tumultuous,
waterfall when he fell
from the highlands
to the underground land of apparent non-existence.

He proved,
that life after life
may become a new birth.

The erudite of
significant understatements
will stay with us
– he's left behind
his and our world.

Translated by Dorota Stępińska

The Stage

Once he had stood on stage,
he realized,
that there were things
that could not be worked out.
Paralysed by the stage fright,
he lost his power.

Although it was not his words
that were supposed to take him
into a magical world,
it was hard for him to prove
that he was a cannibal
and could play someone he wasn't.

He decided
to live away from it,
without criticism or failure.

He didn't think at the time
that there might be those
in front of whom, without pretending,
you did not exist.

Translated by Dorota Stępińska

Temptation

Marked by infirmity
she sates with the light of the body's memory.
Only the imitation of dance
releases apparent happiness.

The world tempts with itself,
and for her it's hard to beat the levels.
At the exhibition
she takes a look at the new collections of shoes.

Only bare,
tireless pigeons
dance
around the trapped life.

Translated by Artur Komoter

William S.
Peters Sr.

Bill's writing career spans a period of over 50 years. Being first Published in 1972, Bill has since went on to Author in excess of 50 additional Volumes of Poetry, Short Stories, etc., expressing his thoughts on matters of the Heart, Spirit, Consciousness and Humanity. His primary focus is that of Love, Peace and Understanding!

Bill says . . .

I have always likened Life to that of a Garden. So, for me, Life is simply about the Seeds we Sow and Nourish. All things we "Think and Do", will "Be" Cause and eventually manifest itself to being an "Effect" within our own personal "Existences" and "Experiences" . . . whether it be Fruit, Flowers, Weeds or Barren Landscapes! Bill highly regards the Fruits of his Labor and wishes that everyone would thus go on to plant "Lovely" Seeds on "Good Ground" in their own Gardens of Life!

to connect with Bill, he is all things Inner Child

www.iaminnerchild.com

Personal Web Site

www.iamjustbill.com

Jean-Michel Basquiat

Even my name is art,
So tell me
What choice did I have

The letters called for me to express,
To paint,
And in my early seeking of understanding
I turned to the streets
Where graffiti was king . . .
And now . . .
Posthumously,
I am also

Read between the lines,
Look earnestly
And you shall see my soul
Baring itself
To the world
Begging for the pain
To stop

And I breathe

Have i lived nobly?
.... not always.
.....
Am I doing so now?
The best I can do is try.

All to often,
We put aside,
Or forget
That which is important
In our little lives

We oft falsely
Inflate ourselves
To be more than what we are,
But this is but
Self-Delusion

We are dependant upon
Illusory things
That we may have something
To which
We afix our values

We say that we are thoughtful,
But that by definition
Is quite different than
Thinking

We say that we care,
That we are considerate,
But even that premise
Is subject to
The tentacles of 'convenience'

Love unequivocally?
Begins within,
But we spend far too much time
Chastising 'Self'
Instead of forgiving
And embracing our
Misgivings and frailties
With compassion and understanding ...
....So how does,
How can one
Truly love another?

When I breathe,
I am inspired
To exhale that
I may breathe again
And feed this machine
Of many needs,
..... More than I am aware of

In my solitude
I sometimes get lucky
And touch my breath
With observance
Hoping that perhaps i
Will discover something
Which is cherishable
Deep within my shallowness
That is worthy of
My continual and staid
Gratitude

Oft times i ponder such things
As 'Wisdom', an elusive anomaly,
But each time I
Contemplate such things

I realize my
Utter foolishness

In the end-game,
(And it is a game)
The forces of existence
Relegate my ambitious self
To an abyss
Where silence and stillness abides,
And all that I am
Is but one breath away
From the next one,
And the next one
Ad infinitum...?
....
Until they are no more ....
Yet ... still
And I breathe.

A Poem in the Making

I want to be lyrical.
I want to be well versed
In the use of a language
That is uplifting,
Informative,
Experiential

I at times wish to rhyme,
Other times not

Some times there is a magic
Hidden in the subterfuge
Of chaos and discordance

I want to transport my readers,
My observers
Into a place, a space
Within themselves
Where a common resonance
Is found between us

I want to heighten our sensitivities
To the fact
That though we are the building blocks
Of this world, this existence,
It and the world remains
Bigger than us

I want to espouse such things,
Such thoughts,
Such emotions
That inspires each of us,
Myself included
To expand, to expand, to expand

I want to invoke thoughtfulness and smiles,
Unmitigated laughter and love,
Contemplation, consideration and compassion

I want to weave and offer
A cloak of humility
That we all can wear

I am searching
For a humanity
That does not falter
When the Sun goes down,
Or when shadows and darkness
Creeps stealthily into our
Sphere of influence

I want to get to intimately know you,
And you, I... the lesser,
And the potential
Of what we collectively
Can become

These things are possible, truly,
For I have read the verse and lyrics
Of others, and
I am truly beyond measure
AMAZED
.....
and i sincerely believe
That not only I,
But we all
Are simply
A Poem in the making.

Isn't that just magnificently grand?

The Butterfly Effect

"IS" in effect

November

2023

Featured Poets

~ * ~

Ibrahim Honjo

Balachandran Nair

Xanthi Hondrou-Hil

Francesco Favetta

i Fly
because I Can
... said the Dreamer to the world.
www.iamjustbill.com

Ibrahim

Honjo

Ibrahim Honjo is a Canadian / Bosnian poet-writer, who writes in Bosnian, and English language. He has worked as an economist, journalist, editor, marketing director, and property manager. He is currently retired and resides in Vancouver, BC.

Honjo is author 24 published books in Serbo-Croatian Language, 7 books in English, 3 books bilingually (in English and Serbo-Croatian language). In addition, 4 joint books of poems published with Serbian poets. His poems have been represented in more than 60 world anthologies, and in more than 40 magazines.

Some of Honjo's poems have been translated in 17 languages. He received several prizes for his poetry.

When A Mountain Climber Dreams

Locked in a painter's body
I revive all colors
all over the luxurious whiteness of the night

I am waiting for Dawn
as the most beautiful mistress
coloured by sunrise
hovering over me
as over that great mountain
under which a tamer of sunlight once lived

the smell of an everlasting flower
paused in my nose
and gorgeous dresses of autumn in a glance
not reaching the breath of my beloved
nor a look in her eyes
in which a cradled dawn sleeps

camping in my eyes is my darling
gentle as silk
hugging the pillow on which I sleep

autumn in my heart is mild and soft
as Chinese silk

the gorgeous mountain Kamikochi
is too far away

my gaze is lost in the night
while Kamikochi sleeps
covered by moonlight

it's time for new ventures

I Missed The Last Flight

The story of clouds
resembles a pigs' dance
with every stop and turn
under a tall tree touching the clouds

a large kite flies above the planet Earth

a bird whispers something to a man

man-cloud closed his eyes
listening to silence coming from the Earth
decomposing dusk to thousands of pieces

space sleeps in its delirium
cunningly silent, preparing retaliation

bird-cloud flew into the unknown

again, I missed the last flight
to an unknown planet

Arrival Out Of Ignorance

For whom the church bells toll
for whom is a muezzin praying from the minaret
on Friday at twelve
for whom I cried that Friday

who are they calling at this time swollen from pain
which I hugged with the first sob

I arrived at the right time, they said
when spring began to mature
they gave me the name of my grandfather
who was swallowed by the great war

all wars are great and blood-stained

I was born after the last great war
I cry for all the wars of the past and future

do the bells toll to announce my birth
or some new great war that will eat me

does the muezzin pray on the minaret
to announce a new upcoming bloodshed
or just advertise my crying

I'm here and I do not know why
my mother did not promise me anything
she only held me on her bosom
tears came out of her eyes
because
she had nothing in her breasts to feed me with

my father was somewhere, carving stone
and he looked on this day through one eye

they promise everyone that it will be better
and it is always better for someone
after great wars

God has never stopped the bloodshed
by brainwashing
they awake the imagination of the population
and with fear, they complete their promises
everything is imagination except my birth

I really did not want to come here
and witness the self-destruction of mankind
somebody planted a cuckoo's egg on me
which I sensed at birth

only my mother and father
rejoiced in my first cry
afterward, everything was according
to the unwritten rules of the universe

it's time to go to that gray stone
and dream in peace
about the peace destroyed
in the name of the Creator of the Worlds
and non-existent democracy

the myth of peace and peacemakers
remains only a myth
because
peace can only be made by producers of war

bells will continue to toll
and a muezzin will pray
sheep will continue to follow a bell-ringer ram

I watch the ship sink without the captain
and the helmsman

I'm singing "The Internationale"

Balachandran

Nair

Balachandran Nair was born in Kerala, India. Nearly thirty years service in Indian Military. A multilingual poet, storyteller and translator. Published four poetry anthologies of his own and contributed poems to more than eighty others. Numerous awards from various literary platforms the world over. Academy Awards from Govt. of Telengana and Govt. of Gujarat, India. Recently created world record by introducing more than three hundred living poets from all over the world and their poems to school children of Kerala as well as introducing more than four hundred students as New Poets to world arena of literature in continuous 365 days of year 2022.

Aging...

Blooming, lotus desires
Sun to come close and pat its cheek
Rowing, wave desires
Land to come close and caress
Blowing, fire desires
Cloud to come close and wick
Dancing, shadow desires
Light to come close and merge
Singing, bamboo desires
Madhav to come close and kiss
Marrying, couple desires
Children to be born and love, get loved
Aging, parents desires
All orphanages to shut close
So that their own children
Won't usher them into,
In pursuit of their own desires!
Because,
Children are difference makers
And different are what they desire!

Xanthi

Hondrou-Hil

Xanthi Hondrou-Hill is a Greek poetess who is multilingual and studied Literature, Public & International Relations Management. She worked for the Greek Consulate in Stuttgart, Germany. In Greece she cooperates with the local municipality of Naoussa, the Archaeological Service of the Prefecture of Imathia and others to create cultural events and festivals. She is an ambassador for literature magazines around the world, like NAMASTE in India and Chinese Literature magazine, Humanity in Russia. She works as journalist for www.faretra.info in Greece.

Eternal Reminder

With the Perfection the sky joins the sea
the signs of Mörike's blue ribbon in the air,
the light of Odysseus Elytis, the peace of Pablo Neruda...
Among blossoming peach and cherry trees wandering speechless

On the mountain tops
with a wild wish of youth in the mind
with a wild herb in the hand
looking down to the hills of natures passion
in breathless excitement

on the pebble beaches with open arms
embracing the width of the horizon
open boarders between countries and continents
overwhelmed by the blossoming breeze
with a poem on the lips, memories in the eyes, marks on the soul

spring is preserved in the hearts
through all seasons
throughout the years and decades
Throughout all our life spring remains
eternal reminder of unstoppable hope

Poetic Habitat

The poets live

in their poems.

They are born in them

they grow up there

they are raised by the words

in the spaces they breath

they are resting on the punctuation

and even when they leave

they exist in the white of every piece of paper

at the edge of every pencil

and in the infinite possibilities of

expression in every language of the world...

Seeds of Peace

In the ceasefires
I plant at the four corners of the horizon
where the blood of my brothers blackens in the sun
seeds of peace.

In the ceasefires I light candles
to light the paths of the spirit
traced and lived by Gandhi.

In the ceasefires I open the door to strangers
to come and share bread, water, roses.
In the ceasefires I build with my hands
the dreams of children
of the whole world.

In the ceasefires I touch
the hearts of those around me
to erase the pain of the past,
to join together to become a circle
To become dance, joy, song.

In the ceasefires I plant
The seeds of my lyrics
To speak in the tongues of the world
to become an eternal hymn for peace

Francesco
Favetta

The poet Francesco Favetta was born in Sicily in Sciacca, he has always loved poetry, writing verses, but above all culture, true culture, food for the soul!

He has written more than 4000 poems so far, he also writes reflections and philosophical thoughts.

In 2018, he was awarded and awarded by the Academy of Sicily : Academician of Sicily.

Sciacca (Sicilia) Italia

The power of poetry

Vibrate in the chest
scream in blood
the verses are the words
it's the breaths sometimes
other times instead
they are sharp knives
it is poetry
the true power of poetry
storm inside the blood.
It's not a game
it is never an empty story
she is always the poem
the words of the soul
the face of human life
love next to thorns
the wind whistling in the sky
daughter of the heart.

It's raining love

It rains love in our hearts
and it's a storm that sweeps away
gray clouds and leaden skies
tired echoes of opaque crystals.
It's raining love in the streets
my breath is still silent
while your caresses are absent
my hands always dig
your wet black eyes
drenched in never dry dew
pearls of love rivulets of light.
It rains love in your cup
of a true and never extinguished woman
it's life that takes you
it is the welcomed miracle
my love given to you
red blood already spilled
that always surprises you
like the roots that bind you
to the story of your wounded heart.
It's raining love and it's a party
it's still raining and it won't stop
we are
two drops of water
that dancing eternally
to the rhythm of bel canto
we settle down gently
on our always lit faces
from true love
never faded
on rainy nights
which have never wet
our souls pure and true.

Of love and heart

Of love
and of reason
of infinite darkness
and of discernment
I would like to talk
to the follies of life
and uncertain thinking
tired footsteps
of lost nostalgia
in the oblivion of the mind
me in spite of everything
I would like to say without words
with the strength of the voice
of my blood
and my tears
imprinted roots
in the immense sea
it's hidden
of my heart
always humble.

Remembering

our fallen soldiers of verse

Janet Perkins Caldwell

February 14, 1959 ~ September 20, 2016

Alan W. Jankowski

16 March 1961 ~ 10 March 2017

Inner Child Press

News

Published Books

by

Poetry Posse Members

We are so excited to share and announce a few of the current books, as well as the new and upcoming books of some of our Poetry Posse authors.

On the following pages we present to you ...

Alicja Maria Kuberska

Jackie Davis Allen

Gail Weston Shazor

hülya n. yılmaz

Nizar Sartawi

Elizabeth E. Castillo

Faleeha Hassan

Fahredin Shehu

Kimberly Burnham

Caroline 'Ceri' Nazareno

Eliza Segiet

Teresa E. Gallion

William S. Peters, Sr.

Now Available

www.innerchildpress.com

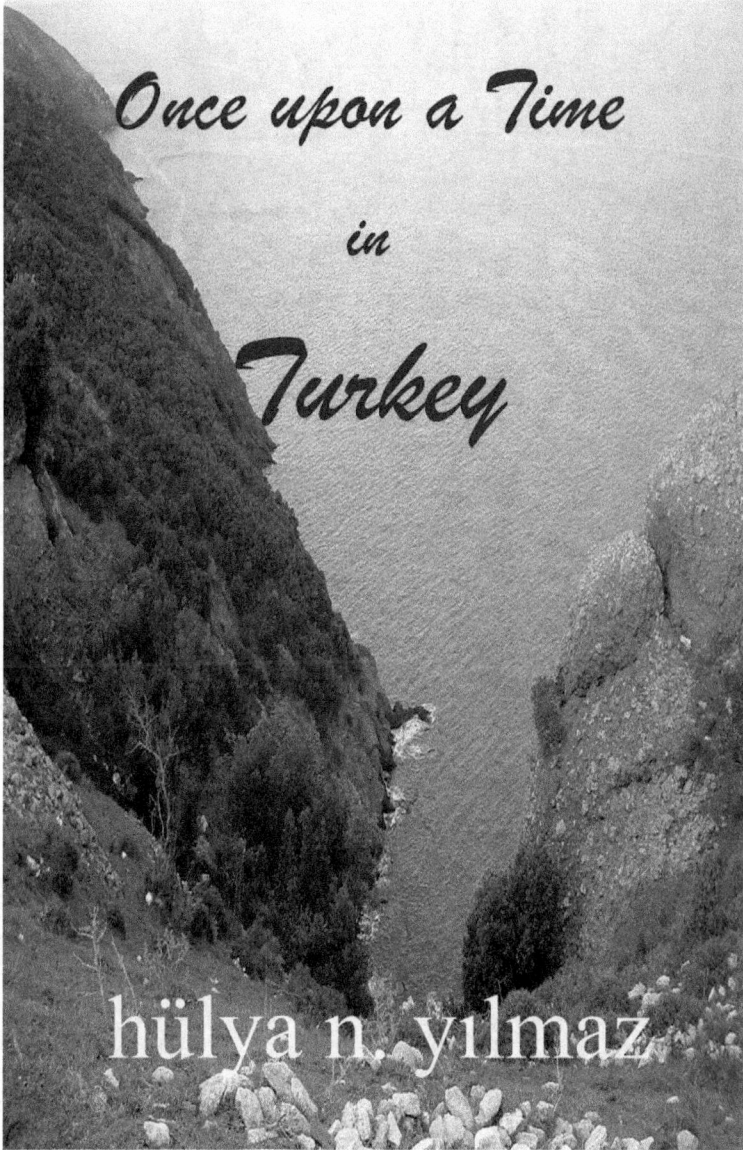

Once upon a Time
in
Turkey

hülya n. yılmaz

Now Available
www.innerchildpress.com

Unapologetically

BLACK

&

Blues

william s. peters, sr.

Now Available

www.innerchildpress.com

Pulling Coats

Shareef Abdur-Rasheed

Now Available
www.innerchildpress.com

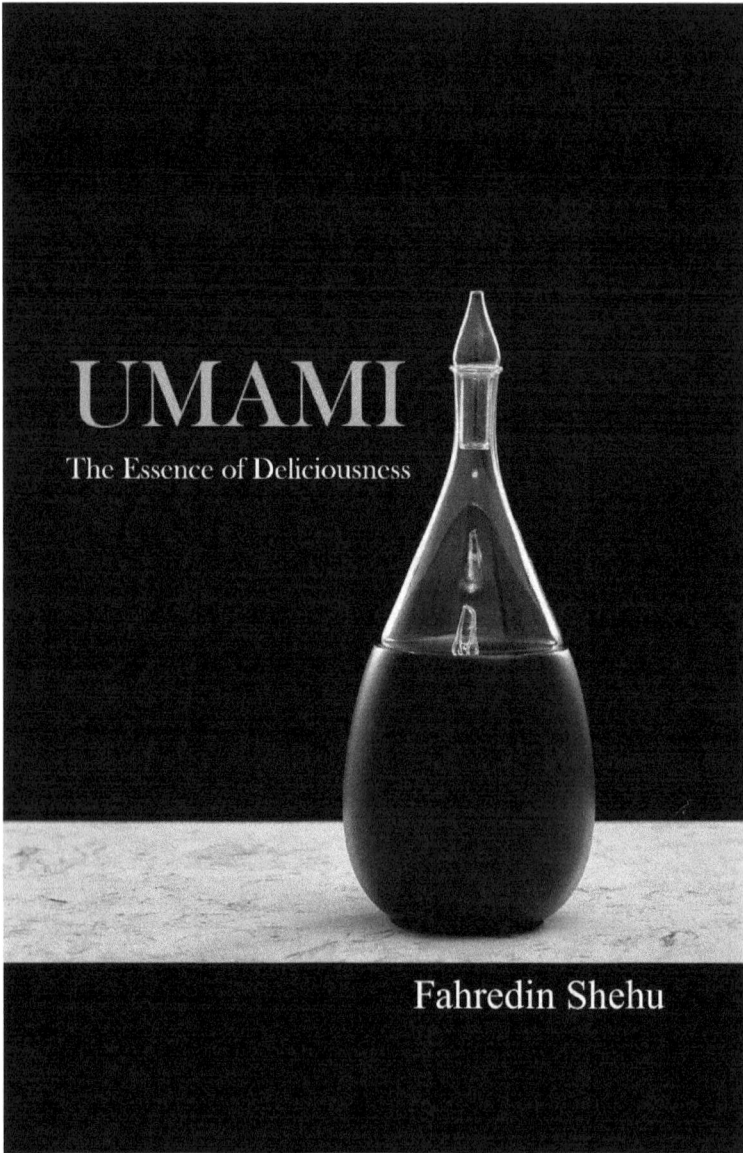

UMAMI
The Essence of Deliciousness

Fahredin Shehu

Now Available
www.innerchildpress.com

After the Frost

Alicja Maria Kuberska

Now Available
www.innerchildpress.com

Fahredin Shehu

ORMUS

Now Available
www.innerchildpress.com

Ahead of My Time

. . . from the Streets to the Stages

Albert *'Infinite'* Carrasco

Now Available
www.innerchildpress.com

151

Eliza Segiet

To Be More

SEARCH FOR THE MAGICAL MULTILINGUAL FROG

A Tale of Ribbit in 50 Languages

KIMBERLY BURNHAM

Now Available at

www.innerchildpress.com

153

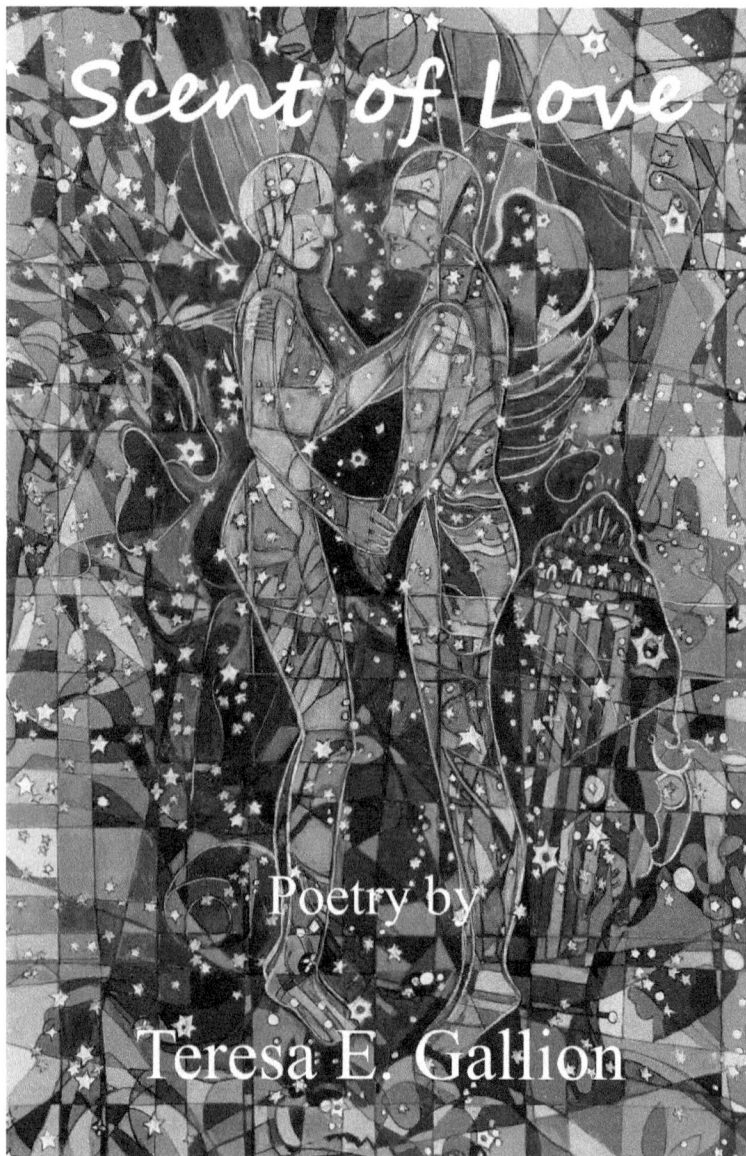

Scent of Love

Poetry by

Teresa E. Gallion

Now Available

www.innerchildpress.com

Inner Reflections
of the
Muse

Elizabeth Castillo

Now Available

www.innerchildpress.com

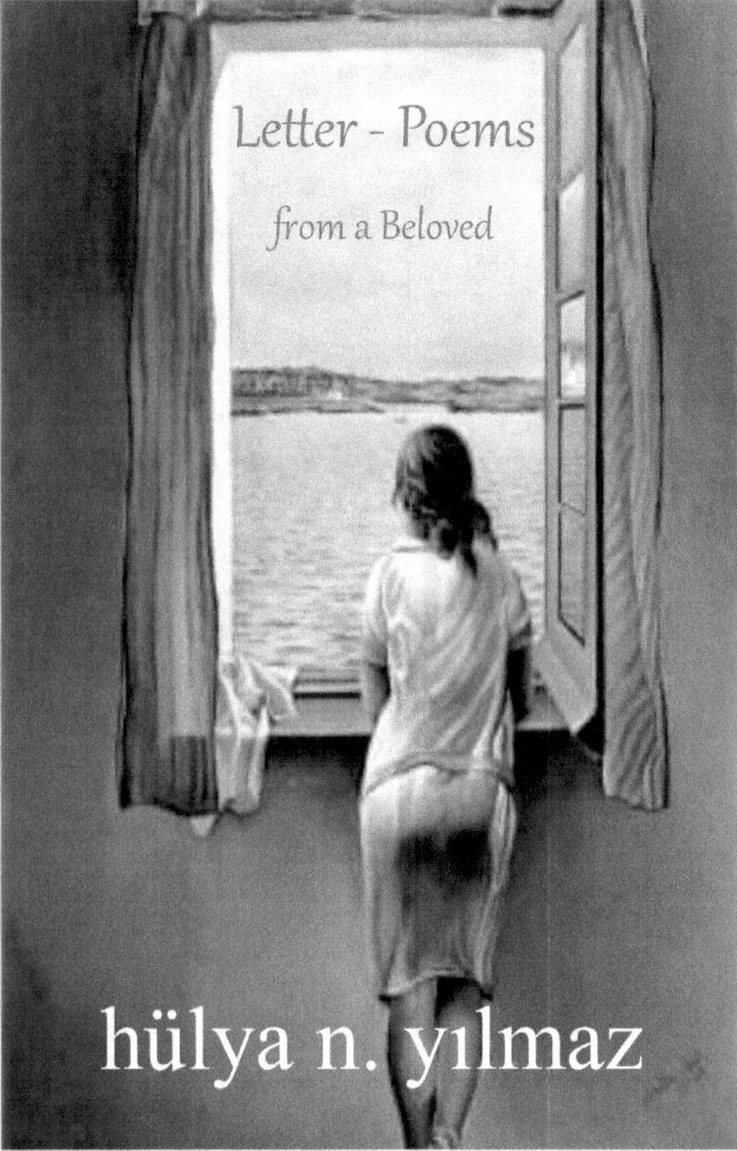

Letter - Poems

from a Beloved

hülya n. yılmaz

Now Available

www.innerchildpress.com

Now Available
www.innerchildpress.com

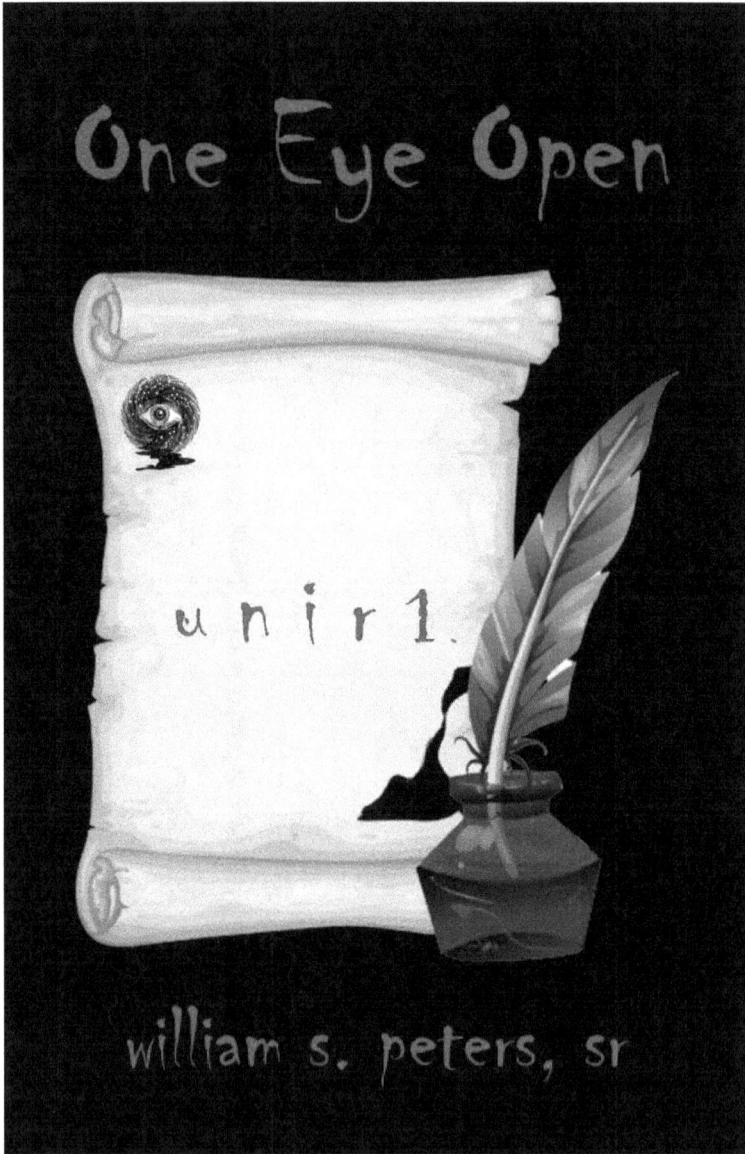

Now Available

www.innerchildpress.com

The Book of krisar

volume v

william s. peters, sr.

Now Available
www.innerchildpress.com

The Book of krisar

Volume I

william s. peters, sr.

The Book of krisar

Volume II

william s. peters, sr.

Now Available

www.innerchildpress.com

The Book of krisar

Volume III

william s. peters, sr.

The Book of krisar

Volume IV

william s. peters, sr.

Now Available

www.innerchildpress.com

Velvet Passions

of

Calibrated Quarks

Caroline Nazareno-Gabis

Now Available

www.innerchildpress.com

Unpaired

Eliza Segiet

Translated by Artur Komoter

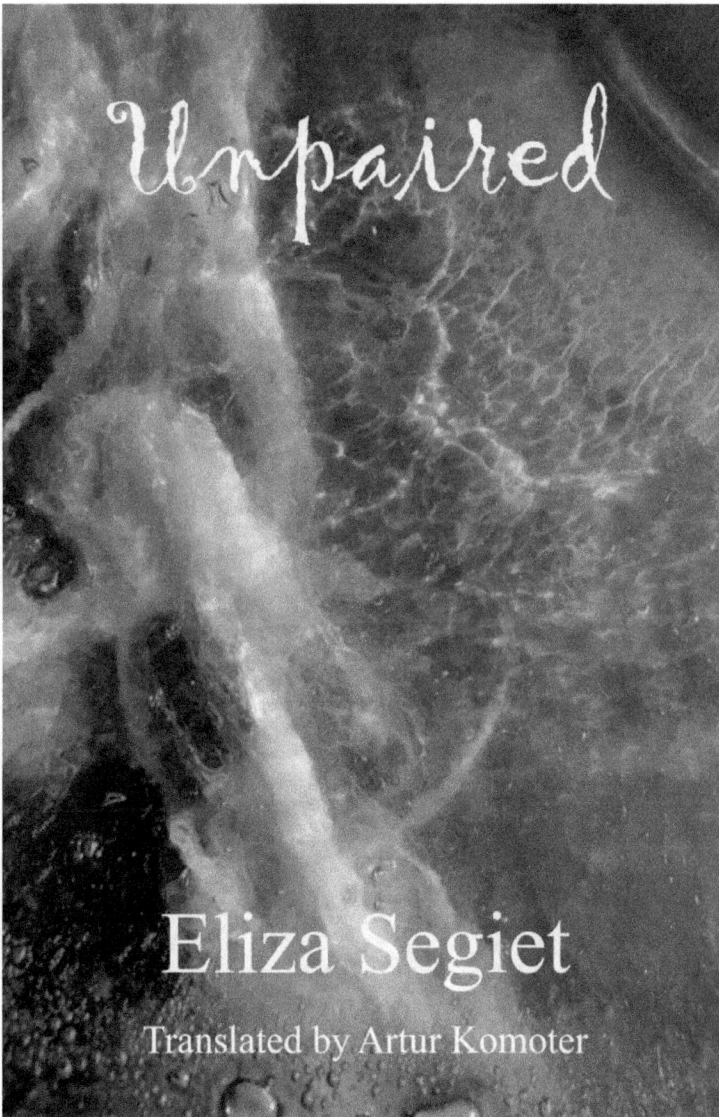

Private Issue

www.innerchildpress.com

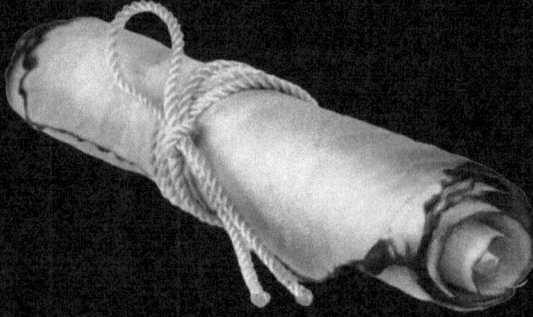

Canlarım
My Lifeblood

poetry in Turkish and English

hülya n. yılmaz

Now Available
www.innerchildpress.com

Butterfly's Voice

Faleeha Hassan

Translated by William M. Hutchins

Now Available at
www.innerchildpress.com

No Illusions

Through the Looking Glass

Jackie Davis Allen

Now Available at
www.innerchildpress.com

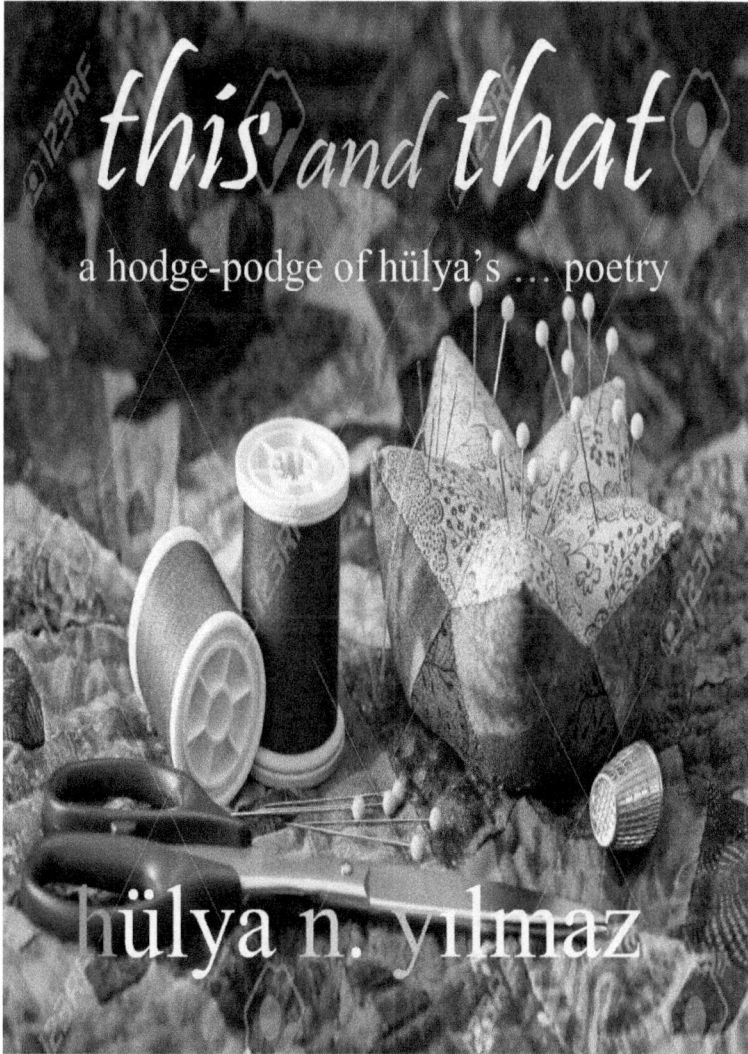

this and that

a hodge-podge of hülya's ... poetry

hülya n. yılmaz

Now Available at
www.innerchildpress.com

Eclectic Verse

mommy i hear those whispers . . . (again)

WilliAM s. PeTers, sR.

Now Available at
www.innerchildpress.com

HERENOW

FAHREDIN SHEHU

Now Available at
www.innerchildpress.com

Magnetic People

Eliza Segiet

Translated by Artur Komoter

Now Available at
www.innerchildpress.com

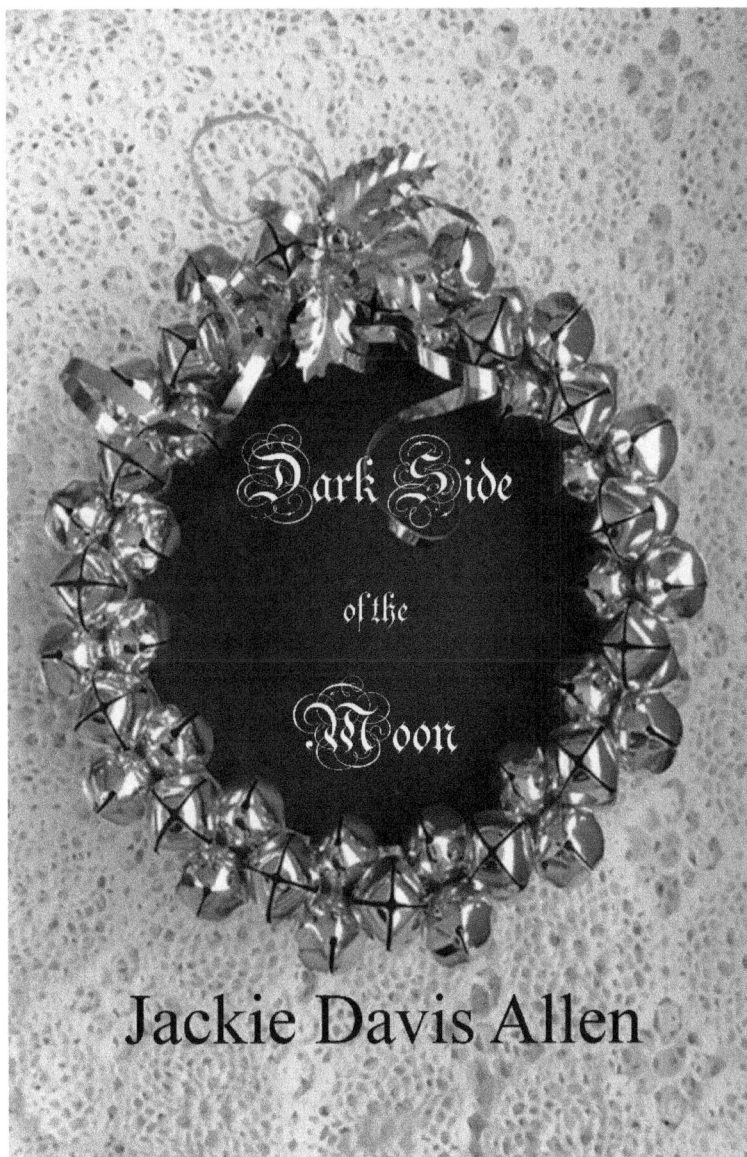

Dark Side

of the

Moon

Jackie Davis Allen

Now Available at
www.innerchildpress.com

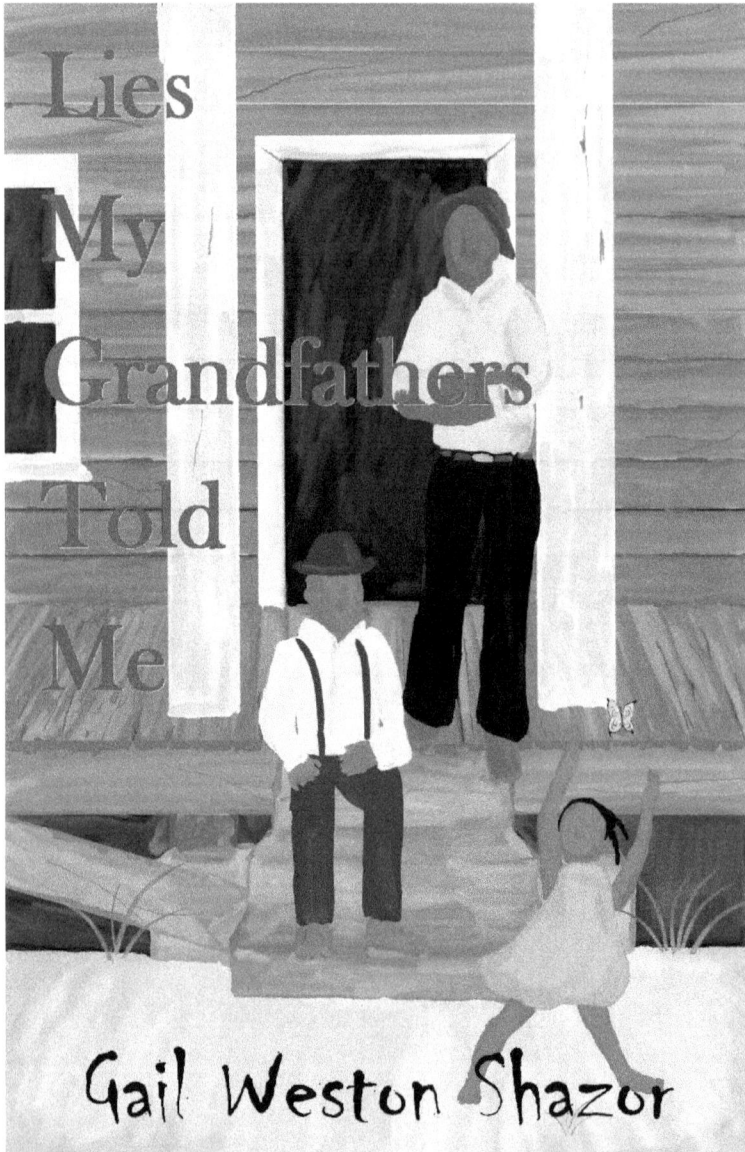

Lies
My
Grandfathers
Told
Me

Gail Weston Shazor

Now Available at
www.innerchildpress.com

Aflame

Memoirs in Verse

hülya n. yılmaz

Now Available at
www.innerchildpress.com

Now Available at
www.innerchildpress.com

Breakfast

for

Butterflies

Faleeha Hassan

Now Available at

www.innerchildpress.com

7 Days
in
Palestine

william s. peters sr.

Now Available at
www.innerchildpress.com

inner child press
presents

Tunisian Dreams

william s. peters, sr.

Now Available at
www.innerchildpress.com

INNER CHILD PRESS

THIS IS WHY I
SLEEP

william s. peters sr.

Now Available at
www.innerchildpress.com

Other

Anthological

works from

Inner Child Press International

www.innerchildpress.com

World Healing World Peace
2020

Poets for Humanity

Now Available

www.worldhealingworldpeacepoetry.com

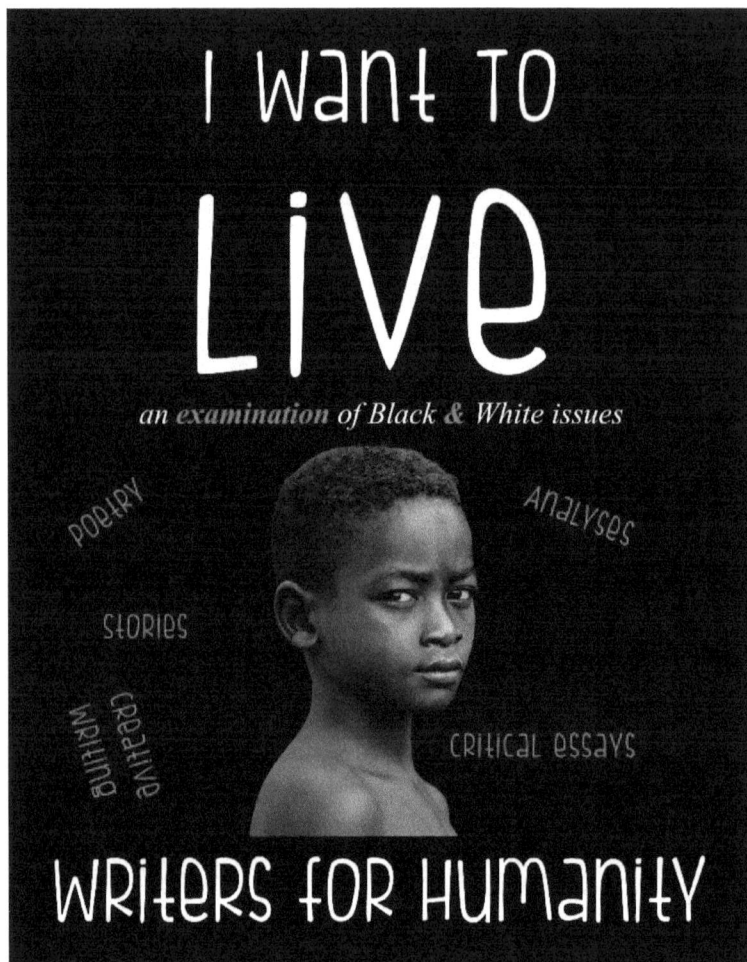

Now Available

www.innerchildpress.com

Inner Child Press International
&
The Year of the Poet
present

Poetry

the best of 2020

Poets of the World

Now Available
www.innerchildpress.com

Inner Child Press International

presents

W.A.R.

We Are Revolution

Poets for Humanity

Now Available

www.innerchildpress.com

the Heart of a Poet

words for a better tomorrow

The Conscious Poets

Now Available
www.innerchildpress.com

Corona

Social Distancing

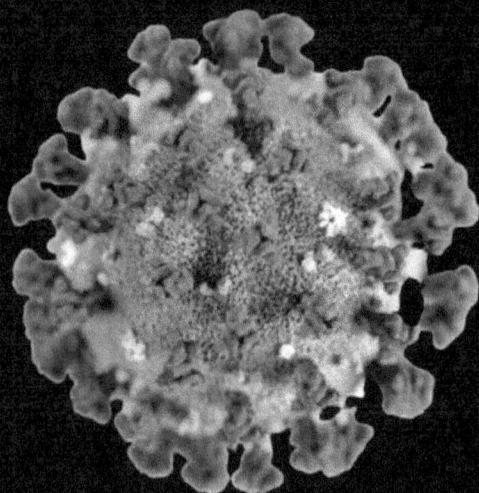

Poets for Humanity

Now Available

www.innerchildpress.com

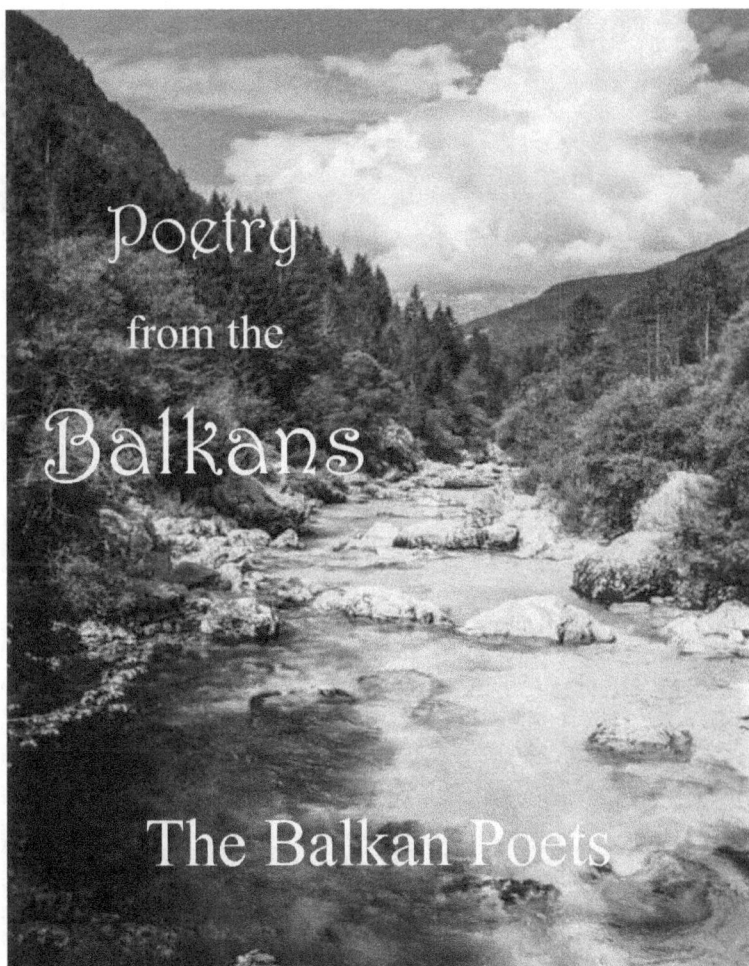

Poetry
from the
Balkans

The Balkan Poets

Now Available at
www.innerchildpress.com

Now Available at
www.innerchildpress.com

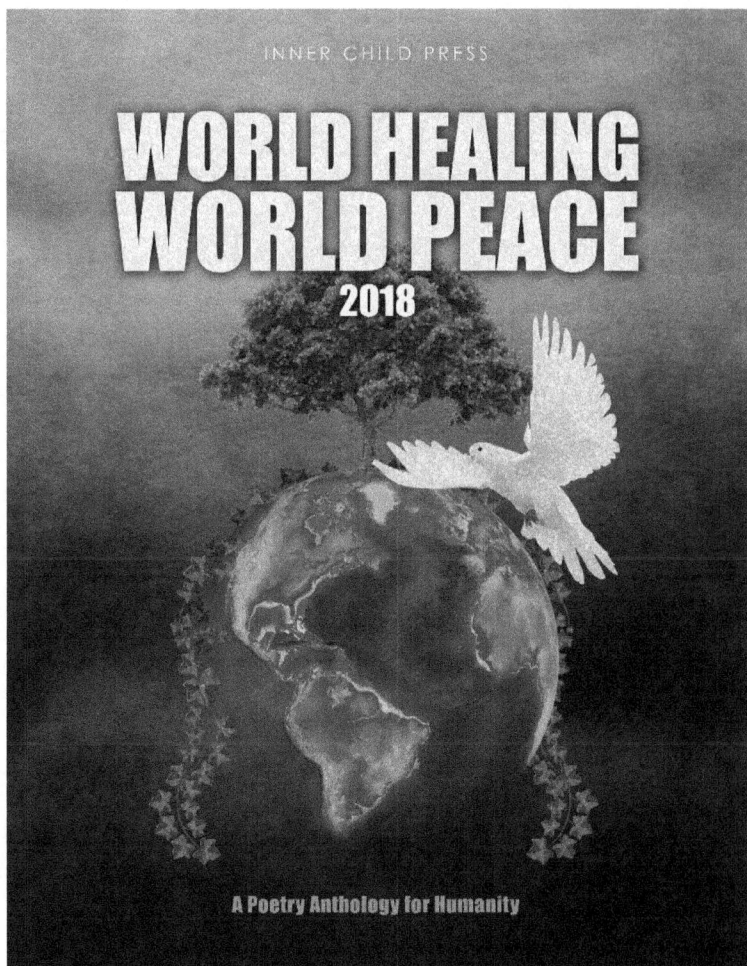

INNER CHILD PRESS

WORLD HEALING
WORLD PEACE
2018

A Poetry Anthology for Humanity

Now Available at
www.innerchildpress.com

Inner Child Press International
presents

A Love Anthology
2019

The Love Poets

Now Available
www.worldhealingworldpeacepoetry.com

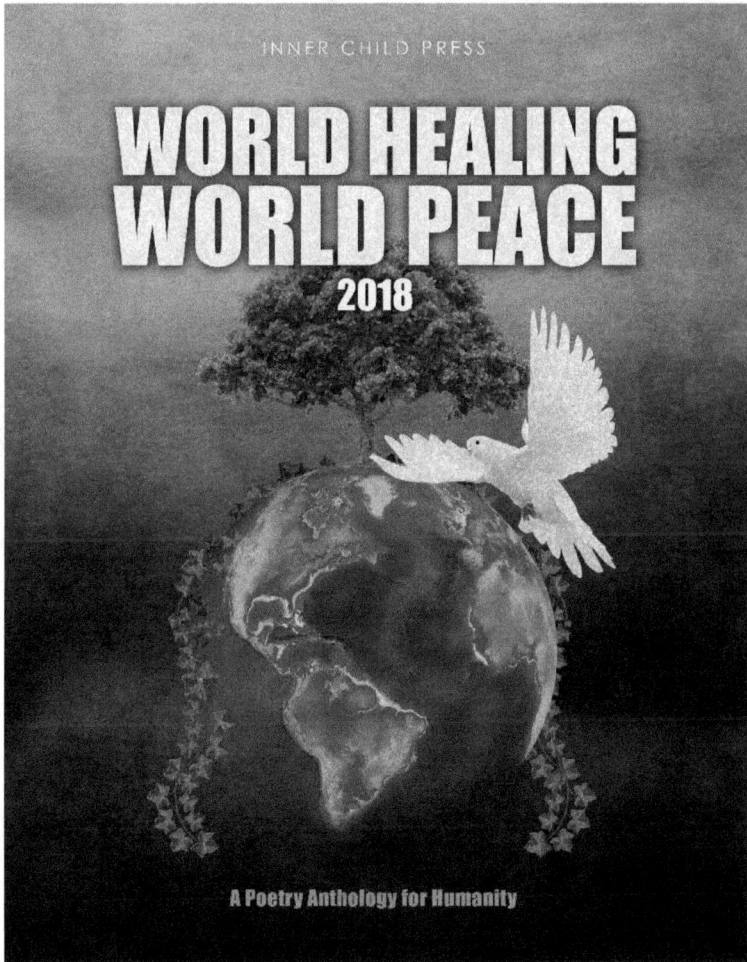

WORLD HEALING WORLD PEACE 2018

A Poetry Anthology for Humanity

Now Available

www.worldhealingworldpeacepoetry.com

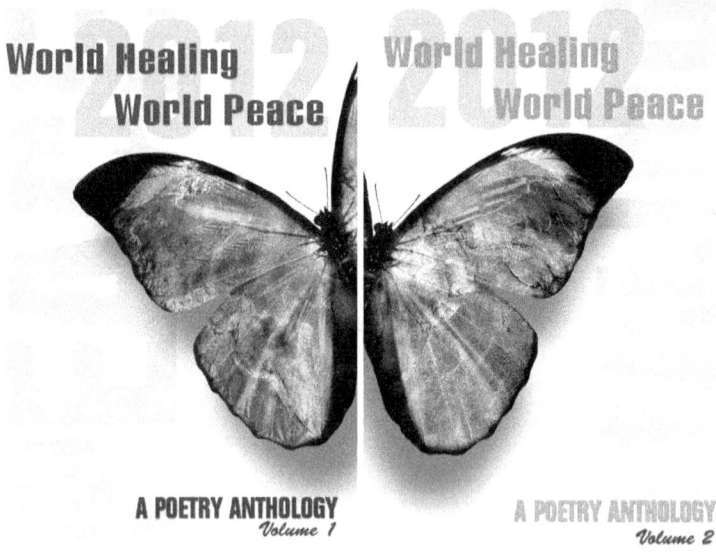

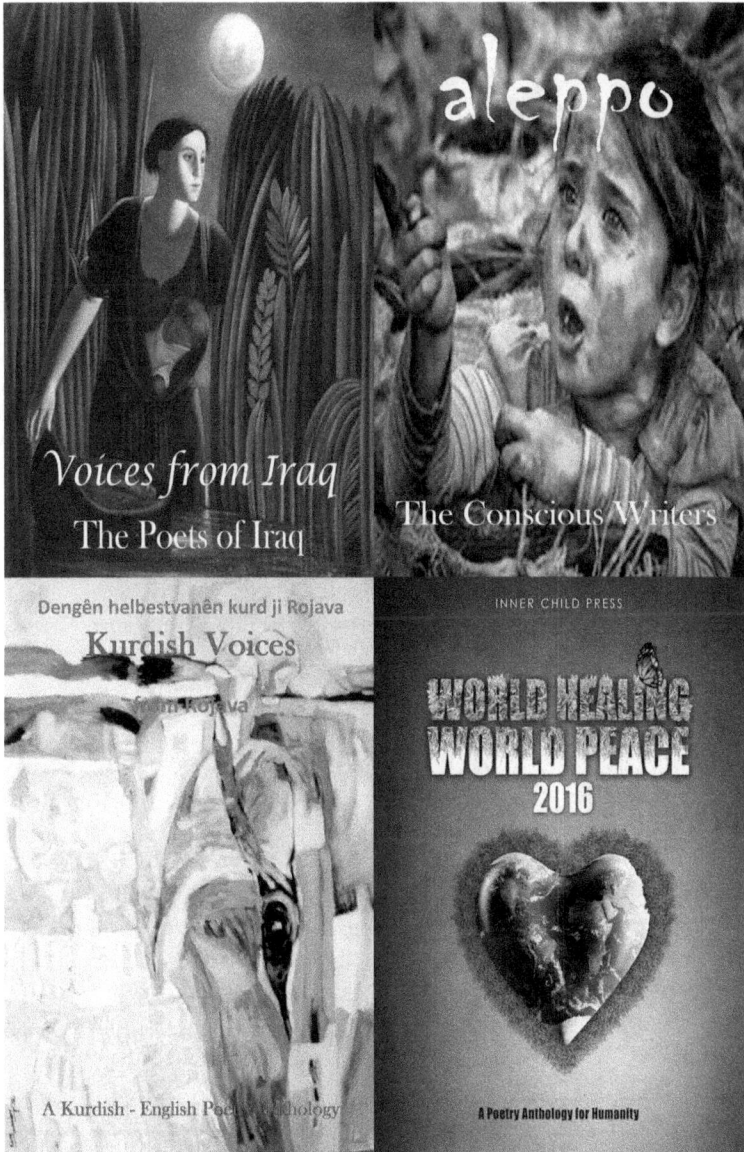

Now Available

Now Available

www.innerchildpress.com/anthologies

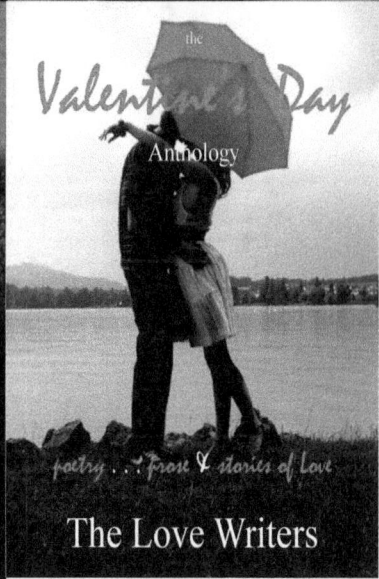

Now Available

www.innerchildpress.com/anthologies

i
want my
PoEtRy
to . . .
a collection of the Voices of Many inspired by . . .
Monte Smith

a collection of the Voices of Many inspired by . . .
Monte Smith
i
want my
PoEtRy
to . . .
volume II

i
want my
Poetry
to . . .   volume 3
a collection of the Voices of Many inspired by . . .
Monte Smith

11 Words
(9 lines . . .)
for those who are challenged
an anthology of Poetry inspired by . . .
Poetry Dancer

Now Available
www.innerchildpress.com/anthologies

The Year of the Poet
January 2014

The Poetry Posse

Jamie Bond
Gail Weston Shazor
Albert 'Infinite' Carrasco
Siddartha Beth Pierce
Janet P. Caldwell
June 'Bugg' Barefield
Debbie M. Allen
Tony Henninger
Joe DaVerbal Minddancer
Robert Gibbons
Neetu Wali
Shareef Abdur-Rasheed
William S. Peters, Sr.

Carnation

Our January Feature
Terri L. Johnson

the Year of the Poet
February 2014

violets

The Poetry Posse

Jamie Bond
Gail Weston Shazor
Albert 'Infinite' Carrasco
Siddartha Beth Pierce
Janet P. Caldwell
June 'Bugg' Barefield
Debbie M. Allen
Tony Henninger
Joe DaVerbal Minddancer
Robert Gibbons
Neetu Wali
Shareef Abdur-Rasheed
William S. Peters, Sr.

Our February Features
Teresa E. Gallion & Robert Gibson

the Year of the Poet
March 2014

The Poetry Posse
Jamie Bond
Gail Weston Shazor
Albert 'Infinite' Carrasco
Siddartha Beth Pierce
Janet P. Caldwell
June 'Bugg' Barefield
Debbie M. Allen
Tony Henninger
Joe DaVerbal Minddancer
Robert Gibbons
Neetu Wali
Shareef Abdur-Rasheed
Kimberly Burnham
William S. Peters, Sr.

daffodil

Our March Featured Poets
Alicia C. Cooper & hülya yılmaz

the Year of the Poet
April 2014

The Poetry Posse
Jamie Bond
Gail Weston Shazor
Albert 'Infinite' Carrasco
Siddartha Beth Pierce
Janet P. Caldwell
June 'Bugg' Barefield
Debbie M. Allen
Tony Henninger
Joe DaVerbal Minddancer
Robert Gibbons
Neetu Wali
Shareef Abdur-Rasheed
Kimberly Burnham
William S. Peters, Sr.

Our April Featured Poets
Fahredin Shehu
Martina Reisz Newberry
Justin Blackburn
Monte Smith

Sweet Pea

celebrating international poetry month

Now Available
www.innerchildpress.com/the-year-of-the-poet

the year of the poet
May 2014

May's Featured Poets
ReeCee
Joski the Poet
Shannon Stanton

Dedicated to our Children

The Poetry Posse
Jamie Bond
Gail Weston Shazor
Albert Infinite Carrasco
Siddartha Beth Pierce
Janet P. Caldwell
Jackie Briggs Rensfield
Debbie M. Allen
Tony Henninger
Joe DaVerbal Minddancer
Robert Gibbons
Neetu Wali
Shameef Abdur-Rasheed
Kimberly Burnham
William S. Peters, Sr.

Lily of the Valley

the Year of the Poet
June 2014

Love & Relationship

Rose

June's Featured Poets
Shantelle McLin
Jacqueline D. E. Kennedy
Abraham N. Benjamin

The Poetry Posse
Jamie Bond
Gail Weston Shazor
Albert Infinite Carrasco
Siddartha Beth Pierce
Janet P. Caldwell
June 'Bugg' Barefield
Debbie M. Allen
Tony Henninger
Joe DaVerbal Minddancer
Robert Gibbons
Neetu Wali
Shareef Abdur-Rasheed
Kimberly Burnham
William S. Peters, Sr.

The Year of the Poet
July 2014

July Feature Poets
Christene A. V. Williams
Dr. John R. Strum
Kolade Olanrewaju Freedom

The Poetry Posse
Jamie Bond
Gail Weston Shazor
Siddartha Beth Pierce
Janet P. Caldwell
June 'Bugg' Barefield
Debbie M. Allen
Tony Henninger
Joe DaVerbal Minddancer
Robert Gibbons
Neetu Wali
Shareef Abdur-Rasheed
Kimberly Burnham
William S. Peters, Sr.

Lotus
Asian Flower of the Month

The Year of the Poet
August 2014

Gladiolus

The Poetry Posse
Jamie Bond
Gail Weston Shazor
Albert Infinite Carrasco
Siddartha Beth Pierce
Janet P. Caldwell
June 'Bugg' Barefield
Debbie M. Allen
Tony Henninger
Joe DaVerbal Minddancer
Robert Gibbons
Neetu Wali
Shareef Abdur-Rasheed
Kimberly Burnham
William S. Peters, Sr.

August Feature Poets
Ann White * Rosalind Cherry * Shaila Jenkins

Now Available

www.innerchildpress.com/the-year-of-the-poet

The Year of the Poet
September 2014

Aster   Morning-Glory

Wild Chicory of September Birthday Flower

September Feature Poets
Florence Malone * Keith Alan Hamilton

The Poetry Posse
Jamie Bond * Gail Weston Shazor * Albert Infinite Carrasco * Siddartha Beth Pierce
Janet P. Caldwell * June 'Bugg' Barefield * Debbie M. Allen * Tony Henninger
Joe DaVerbal Minddancer * Robert Gibbons * Neetu Wali * Shareef Abdur-Rasheed
Kimberly Burnham * William S. Peters, Sr.

THE YEAR OF THE POET
October 2014

Red Poppy

The Poetry Posse
Jamie Bond * Gail Weston Shazor * Albert Infinite Carrasco * Siddartha Beth Pierce
Janet P. Caldwell * June 'Bugg' Barefield * Debbie M. Allen * Tony Henninger
Joe DaVerbal Minddancer * Robert Gibbons * Neetu Wali * Shareef Abdur-Rasheed
Kimberly Burnham * William S. Peters, Sr.

October Feature Poets
Ceri Naz * Rajendra Padhi * Elizabeth Castillo

THE YEAR OF THE POET
November 2014

Chrysanthemum

The Poetry Posse
Jamie Bond * Gail Weston Shazor * Albert Infinite Carrasco * Siddartha Beth Pierce
Janet P. Caldwell * June 'Bugg' Barefield * Debbie M. Allen * Tony Henninger
Joe DaVerbal Minddancer * Robert Gibbons * Neetu Wali * Shareef Abdur-Rasheed
Kimberly Burnham * William S. Peters, Sr.

November Feature Poets
Jocelyn Mosman * Jackie Allen * James Moore * Neville Hiatt

THE YEAR OF THE POET
December 2014

The Poetry Posse
Jamie Bond
Gail Weston Shazor
Albert Infinite Carrasco
Siddartha Beth Pierce
Janet P. Caldwell
June 'Bugg' Barefield
Debbie M. Allen
Tony Henninger
Joe DaVerbal Minddancer
Robert Gibbons
Neetu Wali
Shareef Abdur-Rasheed
Kimberly Burnham
William S. Peters, Sr.

Narcissus

December Feature Poets
Katherine Wyatt* WristenInPen * Santosh Bakaya * Justice Ukaha

Now Available
www.innerchildpress.com/the-year-of-the-poet

202

THE YEAR OF THE POET II
January 2015

Garnet

The Poetry Posse

Jamie Bond
Gail Weston Shazor
Albert 'Infinite' Carrasco
Siddartha Beth Pierce
Janet P. Caldwell
Tony Henninger
Joe DaVerbal Minddancer
Robert Gibbons
Neetu Wali
Shareef Abdur – Rasheed
Kimberly Burnham
Ann White
Keith Alan Hamilton
Katherine Wyatt
Fahredin Shehu
Hülya N. Yılmaz
Teresa E. Gallion
Jackie Allen
William S. Peters, Sr.

January Feature Poets
Bismay Mohanti * Jen Walls * Eric Judah

THE YEAR OF THE POET II
February 2015

Amethyst

THE POETRY POSSE

Jamie Bond
Gail Weston Shazor
Albert 'Infinite' Carrasco
Siddartha Beth Pierce
Janet P. Caldwell
Tony Henninger
Joe DaVerbal Minddancer
Robert Gibbons
Neetu Wali
Shareef Abdur – Rasheed
Kimberly Burnham
Ann White
Keith Alan Hamilton
Katherine Wyatt
Fahredin Shehu
Hülya N. Yılmaz
Teresa E. Gallion
Jackie Allen
William S. Peters, Sr.

FEBRUARY FEATURE POETS
Iram Fatima * Bob McNeil * Kerstin Centervall

The Year of the Poet II
March 2015

Our Featured Poets

Heung Sook * Anthony Arnold * Alicia Poland

Bloodstone

The Poetry Posse 2015

Jamie Bond * Gail Weston Shazor * Albert 'Infinite' Carrasco
Siddartha Beth Pierce * Janet P. Caldwell * Tony Henninger
Joe DaVerbal Minddancer * Neetu Wali * Shareef Abdur – Rasheed
Kimberly Burnham * Ann White * Keith Alan Hamilton
Katherine Wyatt * Fahredin Shehu * Hülya N. Yılmaz
Teresa E. Gallion * Jackie Allen * William S. Peters, Sr.

The Year of the Poet II
April 2015

Celebrating International Poetry Month

Our Featured Poets

Raja Williams * Dennis Ferado * Laure Charazac

Diamonds

The Poetry Posse 2015

Jamie Bond * Gail Weston Shazor * Albert 'Infinite' Carrasco
Siddartha Beth Pierce * Janet P. Caldwell * Tony Henninger
Joe DaVerbal Minddancer * Neetu Wali * Shareef Abdur – Rasheed
Kimberly Burnham * Ann White * Keith Alan Hamilton
Katherine Wyatt * Fahredin Shehu * Hülya N. Yılmaz
Teresa E. Gallion * Jackie Allen * William S. Peters, Sr.

Now Available

www.innerchildpress.com/the-year-of-the-poet

The Year of the Poet II
May 2015

May's Featured Poets

Geri Algeri
Akin Mosi Chinmey
Anna Jakubcza

Emeralds

The Poetry Posse 2015
Jamie Bond * Gail Weston Shazor * Albert 'Infinite' Carrasco
Siddartha Beth Pierce * Janet P. Caldwell * Tony Henninger
Joe DaVerbal Minddancer * Neetu Wali * Shareef Abdur – Rasheed
Kimberly Burnham * Ann White * Keith Alan Hamilton
Katherine Wyatt * Fahredin Shehu * Hülya N. Yılmaz
Teresa E. Gallion * Jackie Allen * William S. Peters, Sr.

The Year of the Poet II
June 2015

June's Featured Poets

Analot Arustamyan * Yvette D. Murrell * Regina A. Walker

Pearl

The Poetry Posse 2015
Jamie Bond * Gail Weston Shazor * Albert 'Infinite' Carrasco
Siddartha Beth Pierce * Janet P. Caldwell * Tony Henninger
Joe DaVerbal Minddancer * Neetu Wali * Shareef Abdur – Rasheed
Kimberly Burnham * Ann White * Keith Alan Hamilton
Katherine Wyatt * Fahredin Shehu * Hülya N. Yılmaz
Teresa E. Gallion * Jackie Allen * William S. Peters, Sr.

The Year of the Poet II
July 2015

The Featured Poets for July 2015
Abhik Shome * Christina Neal * Robert Neal

Rubies

The Poetry Posse 2015
Jamie Bond * Gail Weston Shazor * Albert 'Infinite' Carrasco
Siddartha Beth Pierce * Janet P. Caldwell * Tony Henninger
Joe DaVerbal Minddancer * Neetu Wali * Shareef Abdur – Rasheed
Kimberly Burnham * Ann White * Keith Alan Hamilton
Katherine Wyatt * Fahredin Shehu * Hülya N. Yılmaz
Teresa E. Gallion * Jackie Allen * William S. Peters, Sr.

The Year of the Poet II
August 2015

Peridot

Featured Poets
Gayle Howell
Ann Chalasz
Christopher Schultz

The Poetry Posse 2015
Jamie Bond * Gail Weston Shazor * Albert 'Infinite' Carrasco
Siddartha Beth Pierce * Janet P. Caldwell * Tony Henninger
Joe DaVerbal Minddancer * Neetu Wali * Shareef Abdur – Rasheed
Kimberly Burnham * Ann White * Keith Alan Hamilton
Katherine Wyatt * Fahredin Shehu * Hülya N. Yılmaz
Teresa E. Gallion * Jackie Allen * William S. Peters, Sr.

Now Available
www.innerchildpress.com/the-year-of-the-poet

The Year of the Poet II
September 2015

Featured Poets
Alfreda Ghee · Lonneice Weeks Badley · Demetrios Trifiatis

Sapphires

The Poetry Posse 2015

Jamie Bond * Gail Weston Shazor * Albert 'Infinite' Carrasco
Siddartha Beth Pierce * Janet P. Caldwell * Tony Henninger
Joe DaVerbal Minddancer * Neetu Wali * Shareef Abdur – Rasheed
Kimberly Burnham * Ann White * Keith Alan Hamilton
Katherine Wyatt * Fahredin Shehu * Hülya N. Yılmaz
Teresa E. Gallion * Jackie Allen * William S. Peters, Sr.

The Year of the Poet II
October 2015

Featured Poets
Monte Smith * Laura J. Wolfe * William Washington

Opal

The Poetry Posse 2015

Jamie Bond * Gail Weston Shazor * Albert 'Infinite' Carrasco
Siddartha Beth Pierce * Janet P. Caldwell * Tony Henninger
Joe DaVerbal Minddancer * Neetu Wali * Shareef Abdur – Rasheed
Kimberly Burnham * Ann White * Keith Alan Hamilton
Katherine Wyatt * Fahredin Shehu * Hülya N. Yılmaz
Teresa E. Gallion * Jackie Allen * William S. Peters, Sr.

The Year of the Poet II
November 2015

Featured Poets
Alan W. Jankowski
Bismay Mohanty
James Moore

Topaz

The Poetry Posse 2015

Jamie Bond * Gail Weston Shazor * Albert 'Infinite' Carrasco
Siddartha Beth Pierce * Janet P. Caldwell * Tony Henninger
Joe DaVerbal Minddancer * Neetu Wali * Shareef Abdur – Rasheed
Kimberly Burnham * Ann White * Keith Alan Hamilton
Katherine Wyatt * Fahredin Shehu * Hülya N. Yılmaz
Teresa E. Gallion * Jackie Allen * William S. Peters, Sr.

The Year of the Poet II
December 2015

Featured Poets
Kerione Bryan * Michelle Joan Barulich * Neville Hiatt

Turquoise

The Poetry Posse 2015

Jamie Bond * Gail Weston Shazor * Albert 'Infinite' Carrasco
Siddartha Beth Pierce * Janet P. Caldwell * Tony Henninger
Joe DaVerbal Minddancer * Neetu Wali * Shareef Abdur – Rasheed
Kimberly Burnham * Ann White * Keith Alan Hamilton
Katherine Wyatt * Fahredin Shehu * Hülya N. Yılmaz
Teresa E. Gallion * Jackie Allen * William S. Peters, Sr.

Now Available

www.innerchildpress.com/the-year-of-the-poet

The Year of the Poet III
January 2016

Featured Poets
Lana Joseph * Atom Cyrus Rush * Christena Williams

Dark-eyed Junco

The Poetry Posse 2016

The Year of the Poet III
February 2016

Featured Poets
Anthony Arnold
Anna Chalasz
Sundra Hawthorne

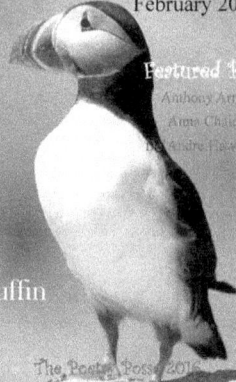

Puffin

The Poetry Posse 2016

The Year of the Poet
March 2016
Featured Poets
Jeton Kelmendi   Nizar Sartawi   Sami Muhanna

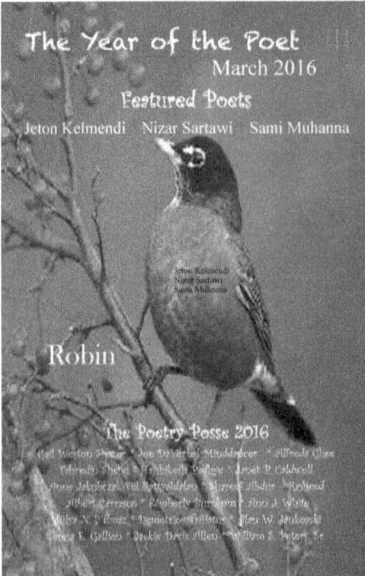

Robin

The Poetry Posse 2016

The Year of the Poet III

Featured Poets

Ali Abdolrezaei

Anna Chalasz

Agim Vinca

Ceri Naz

Black Capped Chickadee

The Poetry Posse 2016

Gail Weston Shazor * Joe DaVerbal Minddancer * Alfreda Ghee
Fahredin Shehu * Hrishikesh Padhye * Janet P. Caldwell
Anna Jakubczak Vel Ratty Adalan * Shareef Abdur - Rasheed
Albert Carrasco * Kimberly Burnham * Ann J. White
Hülya N. Yılmaz * Demetrios Trifiatis * Alan W. Jankowski
Teresa E. Gallion * Jackie Davis Allen * William S. Peters, Sr.

celebrating international poetry month

Now Available
www.innerchildpress.com/the-year-of-the-poet

Inner Child Press Anthologies

Now Available

www.innerchildpress.com/the-year-of-the-poet

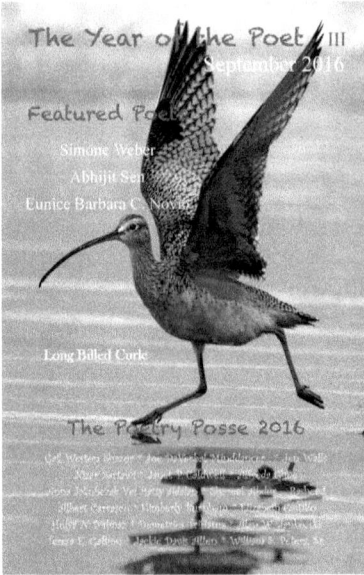

The Year of the Poet III
September 2016

Featured Poets

Simone Weber
Abhijit Sen
Eunice Barbara C. Novio

Long Billed Curlew

The Poetry Posse 2016

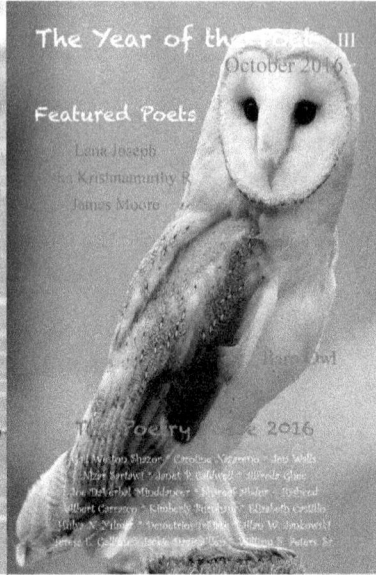

The Year of the Poet III
October 2016

Featured Poets

Lena Joseph
Usha Krishnamurthy R
James Moore

Barn Owl

The Poetry Posse 2016

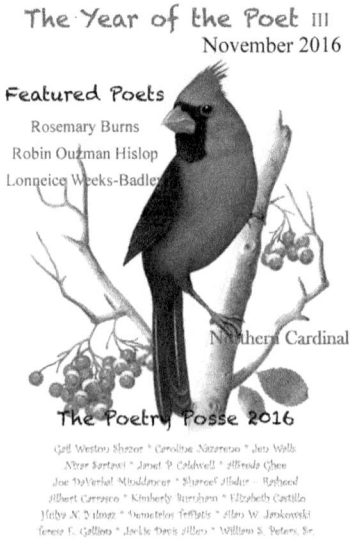

The Year of the Poet III
November 2016

Featured Poets

Rosemary Burns
Robin Ouzman Hislop
Lonneice Weeks-Badley

Northern Cardinal

The Poetry Posse 2016

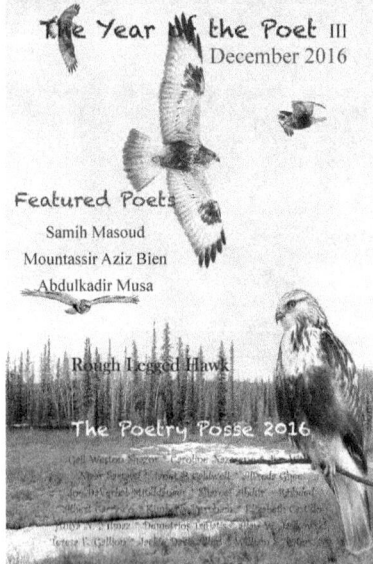

The Year of the Poet III
December 2016

Featured Poets

Samih Masoud
Mountassir Aziz Bien
Abdulkadir Musa

Rough Legged Hawk

The Poetry Posse 2016

Now Available

www.innerchildpress.com/the-year-of-the-poet

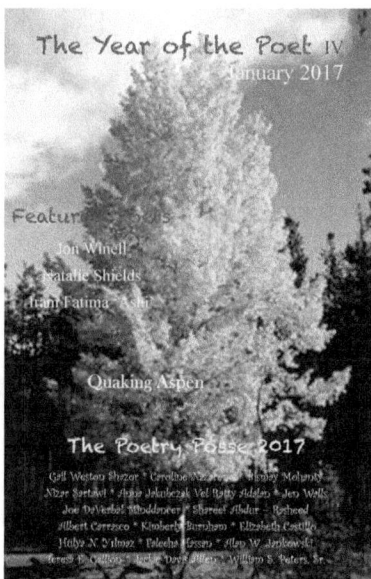

The Year of the Poet IV
January 2017

Featured Poets
Jon Winell
Natalie Shields
Hani Fatima Asin

Quaking Aspen

The Poetry Posse 2017

Gail Weston Shazor * Caroline Nazareno * Bismay Mohanty
Nizar Sartawi * Anna Jakubczak Vel Ratty Adalan * Jen Walls
Joe DaVerbal Minddancer * Shareef Abdur - Rasheed
Albert Carrasco * Kimberly Burnham * Elizabeth Castillo
Hülya N. Yılmaz * Teleaha Hasan * Alan W. Jankowski
Teresa E. Gallion * Jackie Davis Allen * William S. Peters, Sr.

The Year of the Poet IV
February 2017

Featured Poets
Lin Ross
Sohkanta Fathi
Anwer Ghani

Witch Hazel

The Poetry Posse 2017

Gail Weston Shazor * Caroline Nazareno * Bismay Mohanty
Nizar Sartawi * Anna Jakubczak Vel Ratty Adalan * Jen Walls
Joe DaVerbal Minddancer * Shareef Abdur – Rasheed
Albert Carrasco * Kimberly Burnham * Elizabeth Castillo
Hülya N. Yılmaz * Teleaha Hasan * Alan W. Jankowski
Teresa E. Gallion * Jackie Davis Allen * William S. Peters, Sr.

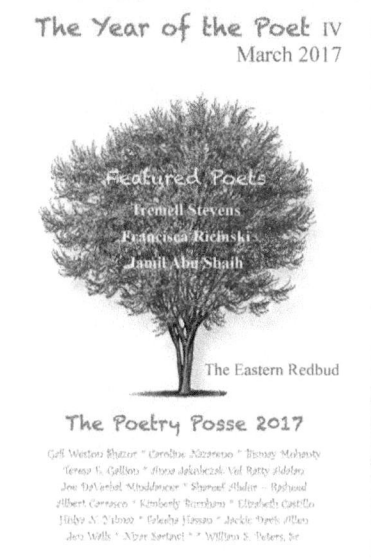

The Year of the Poet IV
March 2017

Featured Poets
Tremell Stevens
Francisca Ricinski
Jamil Abu Shaih

The Eastern Redbud

The Poetry Posse 2017

Gail Weston Shazor * Caroline Nazareno * Bismay Mohanty
Teresa E. Gallion * Anna Jakubczak Vel Ratty Adalan
Joe DaVerbal Minddancer * Shareef Abdur - Rasheed
Albert Carrasco * Kimberly Burnham * Elizabeth Castillo
Hülya N. Yılmaz * Teleaha Hasan * Jackie Davis Allen
Jen Walls * Nizar Sartawi * * William S. Peters, Sr.

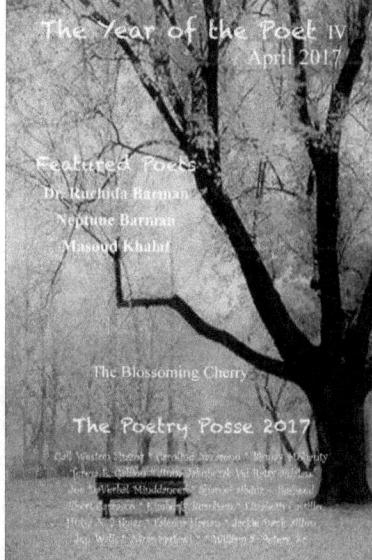

The Year of the Poet IV
April 2017

Featured Poets
Dr. Rachida Barman
Neptune Barman
Masoud Khalaf

The Blossoming Cherry

The Poetry Posse 2017

Gail Weston Shazor * Caroline Nazareno * Bismay Mohanty
Teresa E. Gallion * Anna Jakubczak Vel Ratty Adalan
Joe DaVerbal Minddancer * Shareef Abdur - Rasheed
Albert Carrasco * Kimberly Burnham * Elizabeth Castillo
Hülya N. Yılmaz * Teleaha Hasan * Jackie Davis Allen
Jen Walls * Nizar Sartawi * * William S. Peters, Sr.

Now Available

www.innerchildpress.com/the-year-of-the-poet

The Year of the Poet IV
May 2017

The Flowering Dogwood Tree

Featured Poets
Kallisa Powell
Alicja Maria Kuberska
Fethi Sassi

The Poetry Posse 2017

Gail Weston Shazor * Caroline Nazareno * Tzemin Mahrinty
Teresa E. Gallion * Jhyoti Jakshezak Vel Betty Malvo
Joe DeVerbal Minddancer * Shareef Abdur - Rasheed
Albert Carrasco * Kimberly Burnham * Elizabeth Castillo
Hülya N Yilmaz * Falisha Hosten * Jackie Davis Allen
Jen Walls * Nizar Sartawi * * William S. Peters, Sr

The Year of the Poet IV
June 2017

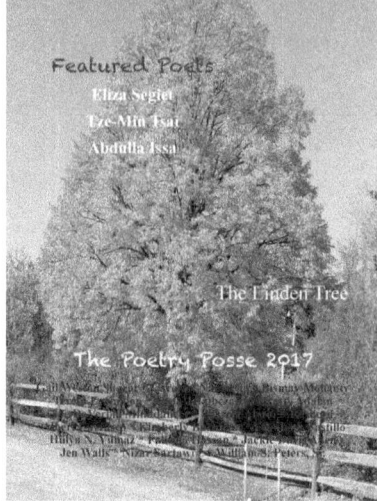

Featured Poets
Eliza Segiet
Tze-Min Tsai
Abdulla Issa

The Linden Tree

The Poetry Posse 2017

Hülya N. Yilmaz * Falisha Hosten * Jackie Davis Allen
Jen Walls * Nizar Sartawi * William S. Peters

The Year of the Poet IV
July 2017

Featured Poets
Anca Mihaela Bruma
Ibaa Ismail
Zvonko Taneski

The Oak Moon

The Poetry Posse 2017

Gail Weston Shazor * Caroline Nazareno * Tzemin Mahrinty
Teresa E. Gallion * Jhyoti Jakshezak Vel Betty Malvo
Joe DeVerbal Minddancer * Shareef Abdur - Rasheed
Albert Carrasco * Kimberly Burnham * Elizabeth Castillo
Hülya N Yilmaz * Falisha Hosten * Jackie Davis Allen
Jen Walls * Nizar Sartawi * * William S. Peters, Sr

The Year of the Poet IV
August 2017

Featured Poets
Jonathan Aquino
Kitty Hsu
Langley Shazor

The Hazelnut Tree

The Poetry Posse 2017

Gail Weston Shazor * Caroline Nazareno
Teresa E. Gallion * Jhyoti Jakshezak Vel Betty Malvo
Joe DeVerbal Minddancer * Shareef Abdur - Rasheed
Albert Carrasco * Kimberly Burnham * Elizabeth Castillo
Hülya N Yilmaz * Falisha Hosten * Jackie Davis Allen
Jen Walls * Nizar Sartawi * * William S. Peters, Sr

Now Available

www.innerchildpress.com/the-year-of-the-poet

The Year of the Poet IV
September 2017

Featured Poets

Martina Reisz Newberry
Ameer Nassir
Christine Fulco Neal
Robert Neal

The Elm Tree

The Poetry Posse 2017

Gail Weston Shazor * Caroline Nazareno * Bismay Mohanty
Teresa E. Gallion * Anna Jakubczak Vel Ratty Adalan
Joe DaVerbal Minddancer * Shareef Abdur – Rasheed
Albert Carrasco * Kimberly Burnham * Elizabeth Castillo
Hülya N. Yılmaz * Faleeha Hassan * Jackie Davis Allen
Jen Walls * Nizar Sartawi * * William S. Peters, Sr.

The Year of the Poet IV
October 2017

Featured Poets

Ahmed Abu Saleem
Nedal Al-Qaeim
Sadeddin Shahin

The Black Walnut Tree

The Poetry Posse 2017

Gail Weston Shazor * Caroline Nazareno * Bismay Mohanty
Teresa E. Gallion * Anna Jakubczak Vel Ratty Adalan
Joe DaVerbal Minddancer * Shareef Abdur – Rasheed
Albert Carrasco * Kimberly Burnham * Elizabeth Castillo
Hülya N. Yılmaz * Faleeha Hassan * Jackie Davis Allen
Jen Walls * Nizar Sartawi * * William S. Peters, Sr.

The Year of the Poet IV
November 2017

Featured Poets

Kay Peters
Alfreda D. Ghee
Gabriella Garofalo
Rosemary Cappello

The Tree of Life

The Poetry Posse 2017

Gail Weston Shazor * Caroline Nazareno * Bismay Mohanty
Teresa E. Gallion * Anna Jakubczak Vel Ratty Adalan
Joe DaVerbal Minddancer * Shareef Abdur – Rasheed
Albert Carrasco * Kimberly Burnham * Elizabeth Castillo
Hülya N. Yılmaz * Faleeha Hassan * Jackie Davis Allen
Jen Walls * Nizar Sartawi * William S. Peters, Sr.

The Year of the Poet IV
December 2017

Featured Poets

Justice Clarke
Mariel M. Pabroa
Kiley Brown

The Fig Tree

The Poetry Posse 2017

Gail Weston Shazor * Caroline Nazareno * Bismay Mohanty
Teresa E. Gallion * Anna Jakubczak Vel Ratty Adalan
Joe DaVerbal Minddancer * Shareef Abdur – Rasheed
Albert Carrasco * Kimberly Burnham * Elizabeth Castillo
Hülya N. Yılmaz * Faleeha Hassan * Jackie Davis Allen
Jen Walls * Nizar Sartawi * William S. Peters, Sr.

Now Available

www.innerchildpress.com/the-year-of-the-poet

The Year of the Poet V
January 2018
Featured Poets

Iyad Shamasnah

Yasmeen Hamzeh

Ali Abdolrezaei

Aksum

The Poetry Posse 2018

Gail Weston Shazor * Caroline Nazareno * Tezmin Iton Tsai
Hülya N. Yılmaz * Faleeha Hassan * Jackie Davis Allen
Teresa E. Gallion * Anna Jakubczak Vel Ratty Adalan
Alicja Maria Kubeńska * Shareef Abdur – Rasheed
Kimberly Burnham * Elizabeth Castillo
Nizar Sartawi * William S. Peters Sr.

The Year of the Poet V
February 2018

Sabean

Featured Poets

Muhammad Azram

Anna Szawracka

Abhilipsa Kuanar

Aamika Aery

The Poetry Posse 2018

Gail Weston Shazor * Caroline Nazareno * Tezmin Iton Tsai
Hülya N. Yılmaz * Faleeha Hassan * Jackie Davis Allen
Teresa E. Gallion * Anna Jakubczak Vel Ratty Adalan
Alicja Maria Kubeńska * Shareef Abdur – Rasheed
Kimberly Burnham * Elizabeth Castillo
Nizar Sartawi * William S. Peters, Sr.

The Year of the Poet V
March 2018

Featured Poets

Iram Fatima 'Ashi'
Cassandra Swan
Jaleel Khazaal
Sharia Zaman

Mexico   Cuba

Caribbean
&
Middle America

The Poetry Posse 2018

Gail Weston Shazor * Nizar Sartawi * Hülya N. Yılmaz
Jackie Davis Allen * Caroline 'Ceri' Nazareno
Alicja Maria Kubeńska * Teresa E. Gallion
Faleeha Hassan * Shareef Abdur – Rasheed
Kimberly Burnham * Elizabeth Castillo
Tezmin Iton Tsai * William S. Peters, Sr.

The Year of the Poet V
April 2018

Featured Poets

The Nez Perce

The Poetry Posse 2018

Now Available
www.innerchildpress.com/the-year-of-the-poet

The Year of the Poet V
May 2018

Featured Poets

Zaldy Carreon de Leon Jr.
Sylwia K. Malinowska
Lindita Ahmeti
Ulelia Priden

The Sumerians

The Poetry Posse 2018

Gail Weston Shazor * Nizar Sartawi * Hülya N. Yılmaz
Jackie Davis Allen * Caroline 'Ceri' Nazareno
Alicja Maria Kuberska * Teresa E. Gallion
Kimberly Burnham * Shareef Abdur – Rasheed
Faleeha Hassan * Elizabeth Castillo * Swapna Behera
Tezmin Ition Tsai * William S. Peters, Sr.

The Year of the Poet V
June 2018

Featured Poets

Bilall Maliqi * Daim Miftari * Gojko Božović * Sofija Živković

The Paleo Indians

The Poetry Posse 2018

Gail Weston Shazor * Nizar Sartawi * Hülya N. Yılmaz
Jackie Davis Allen * Caroline 'Ceri' Nazareno
Alicja Maria Kuberska * Teresa E. Gallion
Kimberly Burnham * Shareef Abdur – Rasheed
Faleeha Hassan * Elizabeth Castillo * Swapna Behera
Tezmin Ition Tsai * William S. Peters, Sr.

The Year of the Poet V
July 2018

Featured Poets

Padmaja Iyengar-Paddy
Mohammad Bilal Hashi
Eliza Segiet
Tom Higgins

Oceania

The Poetry Posse 2018

Gail Weston Shazor * Nizar Sartawi * Hülya N. Yılmaz
Jackie Davis Allen * Caroline 'Ceri' Nazareno
Alicja Maria Kuberska * Teresa E. Gallion
Kimberly Burnham * Shareef Abdur – Rasheed
Faleeha Hassan * Elizabeth Castillo * Swapna Behera
Tezmin Ition Tsai * William S. Peters, Sr.

The Year of the Poet V
August 2018

Featured Poets
Hussein Habasch * Mircea Dan Duta * Naida Mujkić * Swagat Das

The Lapita

The Poetry Posse 2018

Gail Weston Shazor * Nizar Sartawi * Hülya N. Yılmaz
Jackie Davis Allen * Caroline 'Ceri' Nazareno
Alicja Maria Kuberska * Teresa E. Gallion
Kimberly Burnham * Shareef Abdur – Rasheed
Ashok K. Bhargava* Elizabeth Castillo * Swapna Behera
Tezmin Ition Tsai * William S. Peters, Sr.

Now Available

www.innerchildpress.com/the-year-of-the-poet

The Year of the Poet V
September 2018

The Aztecs & Incas

Featured Poets

The Poetry Posse 2018

The Year of the Poet V
October 2018

Featured Poets
Alicia Minjarez * Lonneice Weeks-Badley
Lopamudra Mishra * Abdelwahed Souayah

Bengali

The Poetry Posse 2018
Gail Weston Shazor * Nizar Sartawi * Hülya N. Yılmaz
Jackie Davis Allen * Caroline 'Ceri' Nazareno
Alicja Maria Kubenka * Teresa E. Gallion
Kimberly Burnham * Shareef Abdur – Rasheed
Ashok K. Bhargava * Elizabeth Castillo * Swapna Behera
Tezmin Ition Tsai * William S. Peters, Sr.

The Year of the Poet V
November 2018

Featured Poets
Michelle Joan Barulich * Monsif Beroual
Krystyna Konecka * Nassira Nezzar

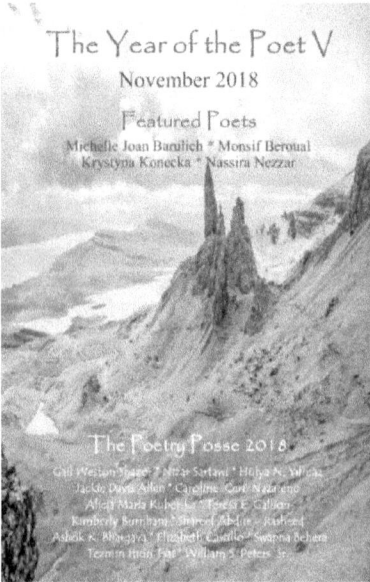

The Poetry Posse 2018
Gail Weston Shazor * Nizar Sartawi * Hülya N. Yılmaz
Jackie Davis Allen * Caroline 'Ceri' Nazareno
Alicja Maria Kubenka * Teresa E. Gallion
Kimberly Burnham * Shareef Abdur – Rasheed
Ashok K. Bhargava * Elizabeth Castillo * Swapna Behera
Tezmin Ition Tsai * William S. Peters, Sr.

The Year of the Poet V
December 2018

Featured Poets
Rose Terranova Cirigliano
Joanna Kalinowska
Sokolović Emir
Dr. T. Ashok Chakravarthy

The Maori

The Poetry Posse 2018
Gail Weston Shazor * Nizar Sartawi * Hülya N. Yılmaz
Jackie Davis Allen * Caroline 'Ceri' Nazareno
Alicja Maria Kubenka * Teresa E. Gallion
Kimberly Burnham * Shareef Abdur – Rasheed
Ashok K. Bhargava * Elizabeth Castillo * Swapna Behera
Tezmin Ition Tsai * William S. Peters, Sr.

Now Available
www.innerchildpress.com/the-year-of-the-poet

The Year of the Poet VI

January 2019

Indigenous North Americans

Featured Poets

Houda Elfchtali
Anthony Briscoe
Iram Fatima 'Ashi'
Dr. K. K. Mathew

Dream Catcher

The Poetry Posse 2019

Gail Weston Shazor * Joe Paire * Hülya N. Yılmaz
Jackie Davis Allen * Caroline 'Ceri' Nazareno
Alicja Maria Kuberska * Teresa E. Gallion
Kimberly Burnham * Shareef Abdur – Rasheed
Ashok K. Bhargava * Elizabeth Castillo * Swapna Behera
Tezmin Ition Tsai * William S. Peters, Sr.

The Year of the Poet VI

February 2019

Featured Poets

Marek Łukaszewicz * Bharati Nayak
Aída G. Roque * Jean-Jacques Fournier

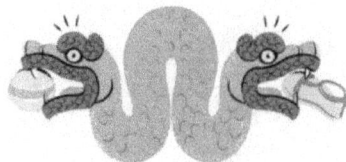

Meso-America

The Poetry Posse 2019

Gail Weston Shazor * Albert Carrasco * Hülya N. Yılmaz
Jackie Davis Allen * Caroline Nazareno * Eliza Segiet
Alicja Maria Kuberska * Teresa E. Gallion * Joe Paire
Kimberly Burnham * Shareef Abdur – Rasheed
Ashok K. Bhargava * Elizabeth Castillo * Swapna Behera
Tezmin Ition Tsai * William S. Peters, Sr.

The Year of the Poet VI

March 2019

Featured Poets

Enesa Mahmić * Sylwia K. Malinowska
Shurouk Hammoud * Anwer Ghani

The Caribbean

The Poetry Posse 2019

Gail Weston Shazor * Albert Carrasco * Hülya N. Yılmaz
Jackie Davis Allen * Caroline Nazareno * Eliza Segiet
Alicja Maria Kuberska * Teresa E. Gallion * Joe Paire
Kimberly Burnham * Shareef Abdur – Rasheed
Ashok K. Bhargava * Elizabeth Castillo * Swapna Behera
Tezmin Ition Tsai * William S. Peters, Sr.

The Year of the Poet VI

April 2019

Featured Poets

DL Davis * Michelle Joan Barulich
Lulëzim Haziri * Faleeha Hassan

Central & West Africa

The Poetry Posse 2019

Gail Weston Shazor * Albert Carrasco * Hülya N. Yılmaz
Jackie Davis Allen * Caroline Nazareno * Eliza Segiet
Alicja Maria Kuberska * Teresa E. Gallion * Joe Paire
Kimberly Burnham * Shareef Abdur – Rasheed
Ashok K. Bhargava * Elizabeth Castillo * Swapna Behera
Tezmin Ition Tsai * William S. Peters, Sr.

Now Available

www.innerchildpress.com/the-year-of-the-poet

The Year of the Poet VI
May 2019

Featured Poets

Emad Al-Haydary * Hussein Nasser Jabr
Wahab Sheriff * Abdul Razzaq Al Ameeri

Asia Southeast Asia and Maritime Asia

The Poetry Posse 2019

Gail Weston Shazor * Albert Carrasco * Hülya N. Yılmaz
Jackie Davis Allen * Caroline Nazareno * Eliza Segiet
Alicja Maria Kuberska * Teresa E. Gallion * Joe Paire
Kimberly Burnham * Shareef Abdur – Rasheed
Ashok K. Bhargava * Elizabeth Castillo * Swapna Behera
Tezmin Ition Tsai * William S. Peters, Sr

The Year of the Poet VI
June 2019

Featured Poets

Kate Gaudi Powiekszone * Sahaj Sabharwal
Iwu Jeff * Mohamed Abdel Aziz Shmeis

Arctic
Circumpolar

The Poetry Posse 2019

Gail Weston Shazor * Albert Carrasco * Hülya N. Yılmaz
Jackie Davis Allen * Caroline Nazareno * Eliza Segiet
Alicja Maria Kuberska * Teresa E. Gallion * Joe Paire
Kimberly Burnham * Shareef Abdur – Rasheed
Ashok K. Bhargava * Elizabeth Castillo * Swapna Behera
Tezmin Ition Tsai * William S. Peters, Sr.

The Year of the Poet VI
July 2019

Featured Poets

Saadeddin Shabin * Andy Scott
Fahredin Shehu * Alok Kumar Ray

The Horn of Africa

Ethiopia   Djibouti

Somalia   Eritrea

The Poetry Posse 2019

Gail Weston Shazor * Albert Carrasco * Hülya N. Yılmaz
Jackie Davis Allen * Caroline Nazareno * Eliza Segiet
Alicja Maria Kuberska * Teresa E. Gallion * Joe Paire
Kimberly Burnham * Shareef Abdur – Rasheed
Ashok K. Bhargava * Elizabeth Castillo * Swapna Behera
Tezmin Ition Tsai * William S. Peters, Sr.

The Year of the Poet VI
August 2019

Featured Poets

Shola Balogun * Bharati Nayak
Monalisa Dash Dwibedy * Mbizo Chirasha

Coexist

Southwest Asia

The Poetry Posse 2019

Gail Weston Shazor * Albert Carrasco * Hülya N. Yılmaz
Jackie Davis Allen * Caroline Nazareno * Eliza Segiet
Alicja Maria Kuberska * Teresa E. Gallion * Joe Paire
Kimberly Burnham * Shareef Abdur – Rasheed
Ashok K. Bhargava * Elizabeth Castillo * Swapna Behera
Tezmin Ition Tsai * William S. Peters, Sr.

Now Available

www.innerchildpress.com/the-year-of-the-poet

The Year of the Poet VI
September 2019

Featured Poets

Elena Liliana Popescu * Gobinda Biswas
Irani Fatima 'Ashi' * Joseph S. Spence, Sr.

The Caucasus

The Poetry Posse 2019

Gail Weston Shazor * Albert Carrasco * Hülya N. Yılmaz
Jackie Davis Allen * Caroline Nazareno * Eliza Segiet
Alicja Maria Kuberska * Teresa E. Gallion * Joe Paire
Kimberly Burnham * Shareef Abdur – Rasheed
Ashok K. Bhargava * Elizabeth Castillo * Swapna Behera
Tezmin Ition Tsai * William S. Peters, Sr.

The Year of the Poet VI
October 2019

Featured Poets

Ngozi Olivia Osuoha * Denise Kondio
Pankhuri Sinha * Christena AV Williams

The Nile Valley

The Poetry Posse 2019

Gail Weston Shazor * Albert Carrasco * Hülya N. Yılmaz
Jackie Davis Allen * Caroline Nazareno * Eliza Segiet
Alicja Maria Kuberska * Teresa E. Gallion * Joe Paire
Kimberly Burnham * Shareef Abdur – Rasheed
Ashok K. Bhargava * Elizabeth Castillo * Swapna Behera
Tezmin Ition Tsai * William S. Peters, Sr.

The Year of the Poet VI
November 2019

Featured Poets

Rozalia Aleksandrova * Orbindu Ganga
Smruti Ranjan Mohanty * Sofia Skleida

Northern Asia

The Poetry Posse 2019

Gail Weston Shazor * Albert Carrasco * Hülya N. Yılmaz
Jackie Davis Allen * Caroline Nazareno * Eliza Segiet
Alicja Maria Kuberska * Teresa E. Gallion * Joe Paire
Kimberly Burnham * Shareef Abdur – Rasheed
Ashok K. Bhargava * Elizabeth Castillo * Swapna Behera
Tezmin Ition Tsai * William S. Peters, Sr.

The Year of the Poet VI
December 2019

Featured Poets

Rohit Kumar (Kumrov) * Sujata Paul
Bharati Nayak * Kapardeli Eftichia

Oceania

The Poetry Posse 2019

Gail Weston Shazor * Albert Carrasco * Hülya N. Yılmaz
Jackie Davis Allen * Caroline Nazareno * Eliza Segiet
Alicja Maria Kuberska * Teresa E. Gallion * Joe Paire
Kimberly Burnham * Shareef Abdur – Rasheed
Ashok K. Bhargava * Elizabeth Castillo * Swapna Behera
Tezmin Ition Tsai * William S. Peters, Sr.

Now Available

www.innerchildpress.com/the-year-of-the-poet

The Year of the Poet VII
January 2020

Featured Poets
B S Tyagi * Ashok Chakravarthy Tholana
Andy Scott * Anwer Ghani

1901 Jean Henry Dunant and Frédéric Passy

The Year of Peace
Celebrating past Nobel Peace Prize Recipients

The Poetry Posse 2020
Gail Weston Shazor * Albert Carasico * Hülya N. Yilmaz
Jackie Davis Allen * Caroline Nazareno * Eliza Segiet
Alicja Maria Kuberska * Teresa E. Gallion * Joe Paire
Kimberly Burnham * Shareef Abdur – Rasheed
Ashok K. Bhargava * Elizabeth Castillo * Swapna Behera
Tezmin Ition Tsai * William S. Peters, Sr.

The Year of the Poet VII
February 2020

Featured Poets
Jennifer Ades * Martina Reisz Newberry
Ibrahim Honjo * Claudia Piccinno

Henri La Fontaine ~ 1913

The Year of Peace
Celebrating past Nobel Peace Prize Recipients

The Poetry Posse 2020
Gail Weston Shazor * Albert Carasico * Hülya N. Yilmaz
Jackie Davis Allen * Caroline Nazareno * Eliza Segiet
Alicja Maria Kuberska * Teresa E. Gallion * Joe Paire
Kimberly Burnham * Shareef Abdur – Rasheed
Ashok K. Bhargava * Elizabeth Castillo * Swapna Behera
Tezmin Ition Tsai * William S. Peters, Sr.

The Year of the Poet VII
March 2020

Featured Poets
Aziz Mountassir * Krishna Paraisa
Hannie Rouweler * Ruzalia Aleksandrova

Aristide Briand ~ 1926 ~ Gustav Stresemann

The Year of Peace
Celebrating past Nobel Peace Prize Recipients

The Poetry Posse 2020
Gail Weston Shazor * Albert Carasico * Hülya N. Yilmaz
Jackie Davis Allen * Caroline Nazareno * Eliza Segiet
Alicja Maria Kuberska * Teresa E. Gallion * Joe Paire
Kimberly Burnham * Shareef Abdur – Rasheed
Ashok K. Bhargava * Elizabeth Castillo * Swapna Behera
Tezmin Ition Tsai * William S. Peters, Sr.

The Year of the Poet VII
April 2020

Featured Poets
Rohini Behera * Mircea Dan Duta
Monalisa Dash Dwibedy * NilavroNill Shoovro

Carlos Saavedra Lamas ~ 1936

The Year of Peace
Celebrating past Nobel Peace Prize Recipients

The Poetry Posse 2020
Gail Weston Shazor * Albert Carasico * Hülya N. Yilmaz
Jackie Davis Allen * Caroline Nazareno * Eliza Segiet
Alicja Maria Kuberska * Teresa E. Gallion * Joe Paire
Kimberly Burnham * Shareef Abdur – Rasheed
Ashok K. Bhargava * Elizabeth Castillo * Swapna Behera
Tezmin Ition Tsai * William S. Peters, Sr.

Now Available

www.innerchildpress.com/the-year-of-the-poet

The Year of the Poet VII
May 2020

Featured Poets
Alok Kumar Ray * Eden S. Trinidad
Franco Barbato * Izabela Zubko

Ralph Bunche ~ 1950

The Year of Peace
Celebrating past Nobel Peace Prize Recipients

The Poetry Posse 2020
Gail Weston Shazor * Albert Carasco * Hülya N. Yılmaz
Jackie Davis Allen * Caroline Nazareno * Eliza Segiet
Alicja Maria Kuberska * Teresa E. Gallion * Joe Paire
Kimberly Burnham * Shareef Abdur – Rasheed
Ashok K. Bhargava * Elizabeth Castillo * Swapna Behera
Tezmin Ition Tsai * William S. Peters, Sr.

The Year of the Poet VII
June 2020

Featured Poets
Eftichia Kapardeli * Metin Cengiz
Hussein Habasch * Kosh K Mathew

Albert John Lutuli ~ 1960

The Year of Peace
Celebrating past Nobel Peace Prize Recipients

The Poetry Posse 2020
Gail Weston Shazor * Albert Carasco * Hülya N. Yılmaz
Jackie Davis Allen * Caroline Nazareno * Eliza Segiet
Alicja Maria Kuberska * Teresa E. Gallion * Joe Paire
Kimberly Burnham * Shareef Abdur – Rasheed
Ashok K. Bhargava * Elizabeth Castillo * Swapna Behera
Tezmin Ition Tsai * William S. Peters, Sr.

The Year of the Poet VII
July 2020

Featured Poets
Mykola Martyniuk * Orbindu Ganga
Roula Pollard * Karn Praktisha

Norman Ernest Borlaug ~ 1970

The Year of Peace
Celebrating past Nobel Peace Prize Recipients

The Poetry Posse 2020
Gail Weston Shazor * Albert Carasco * Hülya N. Yılmaz
Jackie Davis Allen * Caroline Nazareno * Eliza Segiet
Alicja Maria Kuberska * Teresa E. Gallion * Joe Paire
Kimberly Burnham * Shareef Abdur – Rasheed
Ashok K. Bhargava * Elizabeth Castillo * Swapna Behera
Tezmin Ition Tsai * William S. Peters, Sr.

The Year of the Poet VII
August 2020

Featured Poets
Dr Pragya Suman * Chinh Nguyen
Srinivas Vasudev * Ugwu Leonard Ifeanyi, Jr.

Adolfo Pérez Esquivel ~ 1980

The Year of Peace
Celebrating past Nobel Peace Prize Recipients

The Poetry Posse 2020
Gail Weston Shazor * Albert Carasco * Hülya N. Yılmaz
Jackie Davis Allen * Caroline Nazareno * Eliza Segiet
Alicja Maria Kuberska * Teresa E. Gallion * Joe Paire
Kimberly Burnham * Shareef Abdur – Rasheed
Ashok K. Bhargava * Elizabeth Castillo * Swapna Behera
Tezmin Ition Tsai * William S. Peters, Sr.

Now Available
www.innerchildpress.com/the-year-of-the-poet

The Year of the Poet VII
September 2020
Featured Poets
Raed Anis Al-Jishi * Sokrosovic Sinclane
Dr. Brajesh Kumar Gupta * Umid Najjari

Mikhail Sergeyevich Gorbachev ~ 1990

The Year of Peace
Celebrating past Nobel Peace Prize Recipients

The Poetry Posse 2020
Gail Weston Sharor * Albert Carasco * Hülya N. Yılmaz
Jackie Davis Allen * Caroline Nazareno * Eliza Segiet
Alicja Maria Kuberska * Teresa E. Gallion * Joe Paire
Kimberly Burnham * Shareef Abdur – Rasheed
Ashok K. Bhargava * Elizabeth Castillo * Swapna Behera
Tezmin Ition Tsai * William S. Peters, Sr.

The Year of the Poet VII
October 2020
Featured Poets
Mutawaf A. Shaheed * Galina Italyanskaya
Nadeem Fraz * Avril Tanya Meallem

Kim Dae-jung ~ 2000

The Year of Peace
Celebrating past Nobel Peace Prize Recipients

The Poetry Posse 2020
Gail Weston Sharor * Albert Carasco * Hülya N. Yılmaz
Jackie Davis Allen * Caroline Nazareno * Eliza Segiet
Alicja Maria Kuberska * Teresa E. Gallion * Joe Paire
Kimberly Burnham * Shareef Abdur – Rasheed
Ashok K. Bhargava * Elizabeth Castillo * Swapna Behera
Tezmin Ition Tsai * William S. Peters, Sr.

The Year of the Poet VII
November 2020
Featured Poets
Elisa Mascia * Sue Lindenberg McClelland
Hanif Janubi * Ivan Gacina

Liu Xiaobo ~ 2010

The Year of Peace
Celebrating past Nobel Peace Prize Recipients

The Poetry Posse 2020
Gail Weston Sharor * Albert Carasco * Hülya N. Yılmaz
Jackie Davis Allen * Caroline Nazareno * Eliza Segiet
Alicja Maria Kuberska * Teresa E. Gallion * Joe Paire
Kimberly Burnham * Shareef Abdur – Rasheed
Ashok K. Bhargava * Elizabeth Castillo * Swapna Behera
Tezmin Ition Tsai * William S. Peters, Sr.

The Year of the Poet VII
December 2020
Featured Poets
Ratan Ghosh * Ibtisam Ibrahim Al-Asady
Brindha Vinodh * Selma Kopic

Abiy Ahmed Ali ~ 2019

The Year of Peace
Celebrating past Nobel Peace Prize Recipients

The Poetry Posse 2020
Gail Weston Shazor * Albert Carasco * Hülya N. Yılmaz
Jackie Davis Allen * Caroline Nazareno * Eliza Segiet
Alicja Maria Kuberska * Teresa E. Gallion * Joe Paire
Kimberly Burnham * Shareef Abdur – Rasheed
Ashok K. Bhargava * Elizabeth Castillo * Swapna Behera
Tezmin Ition Tsai * William S. Peters, Sr.

Now Available
www.innerchildpress.com/the-year-of-the-poet

The Year of the Poet VIII
January 2021

Featured Global Poets

Andrew Scott * Debaprasanna Biswas
Shakil Kalam * Changming Yuan

Banksy's The Girl with the Pierced Eardrum

Poetry ... Ekphrasticly Speaking
The Poetry Posse 2020

Gail Weston Shazor * Albert Carasco * Hülya N. Yılmaz
Jackie Davis Allen * Caroline Nazareno * Eliza Segiet
Alicja Maria Kuberska * Teresa E. Gallion * Joe Paire
Kimberly Burnham * Shareef Abdur – Rasheed
Ashok K. Bhargava * Elizabeth Castillo * Swapna Behera
Tezmin Ition Tsai * William S. Peters, Sr.

The Year of the Poet VIII
February 2021

Featured Global Poets

T. Ramesh Babu * Ruchida Barman
Neptune Barman * Faleeha Hassan

Emory Douglas : 1968 Olympics mural

Poetry ... Ekphrasticly Speaking
The Poetry Posse 2021

Gail Weston Shazor * Albert Carasco * Hülya N. Yılmaz
Jackie Davis Allen * Caroline Nazareno * Eliza Segiet
Alicja Maria Kuberska * Teresa E. Gallion * Joe Paire
Kimberly Burnham * Shareef Abdur – Rasheed
Ashok K. Bhargava * Elizabeth Castillo * Swapna Behera
Tezmin Ition Tsai * William S. Peters, Sr.

The Year of the Poet VIII
March 2021

Featured Global Poets

Claudia Piccinno * Mohammed Jabr
Luzviminda Rivera *Nigar Arif

Tatyana Fazlalizadeh

Poetry ... Ekphrasticly Speaking
The Poetry Posse 2021

Gail Weston Shazor * Albert Carasco * Hülya N. Yılmaz
Jackie Davis Allen * Caroline Nazareno * Eliza Segiet
Alicja Maria Kuberska * Teresa E. Gallion * Joe Paire
Kimberly Burnham * Shareef Abdur – Rasheed
Ashok K. Bhargava * Elizabeth Castillo * Swapna Behera
Tezmin Ition Tsai * William S. Peters, Sr.

The Year of the Poet VIII
April 2021

Featured Global Poets

Katarzyna Brus- Sawczuk * Anwesha Paul
Rozalia Aleksandrova * Shahid Abbas

Pablo O'Higgins

Poetry ... Ekphrasticly Speaking
The Poetry Posse 2021

Gail Weston Shazor * Albert Carasco * Hülya N. Yılmaz
Jackie Davis Allen * Caroline Nazareno * Eliza Segiet
Alicja Maria Kuberska * Teresa E. Gallion * Joe Paire
Kimberly Burnham * Shareef Abdur – Rasheed
Ashok K. Bhargava * Elizabeth Castillo * Swapna Behera
Tezmin Ition Tsai * William S. Peters, Sr

Now Available

www.innerchildpress.com/the-year-of-the-poet

The Year of the Poet VIII

May 2021

Featured Global Poets

Paramita Mukherjee Mullick * Rose Zerguine
Jaydeep Sarangi * Bismay Mohanty

Diego Rivera

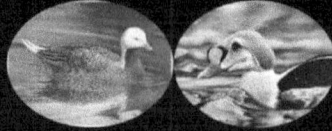

Poetry ... Ekphrasticly Speaking

The Poetry Posse 2021

Gail Weston Shazor * Albert Carasco * Hülya N. Yılmaz
Jackie Davis Allen * Caroline Nazareno * Eliza Segiet
Alicja Maria Kuberska * Teresa E. Gallion * Joe Paire
Kimberly Burnham * Shareef Abdur – Rasheed
Ashok K. Bhargava * Elizabeth Castillo * Swapna Behera
Tezmin Ition Tsai * William S. Peters, Sr.

The Year of the Poet VIII

June 2021

Featured Global Poets

Alonzo "zO" Gross * Lali Tsipi Michaeli
Tareq al Karmy * Tirthendu Ganguly

Rayen Kang

Poetry ... Ekphrasticly Speaking

The Poetry Posse 2021

Gail Weston Shazor * Albert Carasco * Hülya N. Yılmaz
Jackie Davis Allen * Caroline Nazareno * Eliza Segiet
Alicja Maria Kuberska * Teresa E. Gallion * Joe Paire
Kimberly Burnham * Shareef Abdur – Rasheed
Ashok K. Bhargava * Elizabeth Castillo * Swapna Behera
Tezmin Ition Tsai * William S. Peters, Sr.

The Year of the Poet VIII

July 2021

Featured Global Poets

Iram Jaan * Vesna Mundishevska-Veljanovska
Ngozi Olivia Osuoha * Lan Qyqalla

Goncalao Mabunda

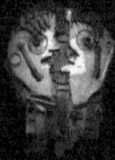

Poetry ... Ekphrasticly Speaking

The Poetry Posse 2021

Gail Weston Shazor * Albert Carasco * Hülya N. Yılmaz
Jackie Davis Allen * Caroline Nazareno * Eliza Segiet
Alicja Maria Kuberska * Teresa E. Gallion * Joe Paire
Kimberly Burnham * Shareef Abdur – Rasheed
Ashok K. Bhargava * Elizabeth Castillo * Swapna Behera
Tezmin Ition Tsai * William S. Peters, Sr.

The Year of the Poet VIII

August 2021

Featured Global Poets

Caroline Laurent Turunc * Kamal Dhungana
Pankhuri Sinha * Paramita Mukherjee Mullick

Mundara Koorang

Poetry ... Ekphrasticly Speaking

The Poetry Posse 2021

Gail Weston Shazor * Albert Carasco * Hülya N. Yılmaz
Jackie Davis Allen * Caroline Nazareno * Eliza Segiet
Alicja Maria Kuberska * Teresa E. Gallion * Joe Paire
Kimberly Burnham * Shareef Abdur – Rasheed
Ashok K. Bhargava * Elizabeth Castillo * Swapna Behera
Tezmin Ition Tsai * William S. Peters, Sr.

Now Available

www.innerchildpress.com/the-year-of-the-poet

The Year of the Poet VIII

September 2021

Featured Global Poets

Monsif Beroual * Sandesh Ghimire

Sharmila Poudel * Pavol Janik

Heather Jansch

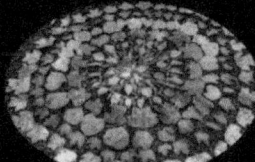

Poetry ... Ekphrasticly Speaking

The Poetry Posse 2021

Gail Weston Shazor * Albert Carasco * Hülya N. Yılmaz
Jackie Davis Allen * Caroline Nazareno * Eliza Segiet
Alicja Maria Kuberska * Teresa E. Gallion * Joe Paire
Kimberly Burnham * Shareef Abdur – Rasheed
Ashok K. Bhargava * Elizabeth Castillo * Swapna Behera
Tezmin Ition Tsai * William S. Peters, Sr.

The Year of the Poet VIII

October 2021

Featured Global Poets

C. E. Shy * Saswata Ganguly

Suranjit Gain * Hasiba Hilal

Dale Lamphere

Poetry ... Ekphrasticly Speaking

The Poetry Posse 2021

Gail Weston Shazor * Albert Carasco * Hülya N. Yılmaz
Jackie Davis Allen * Caroline Nazareno * Eliza Segiet
Alicja Maria Kuberska * Teresa E. Gallion * Joe Paire
Kimberly Burnham * Shareef Abdur – Rasheed
Ashok K. Bhargava * Elizabeth Castillo * Swapna Behera
Tezmin Ition Tsai * William S. Peters, Sr.

The Year of the Poet VIII

November 2021

Featured Global Poets

Errol D. Bean * Ibrahim Honjo

Tanja Ajtic * Rajashree Mohapatra

Andy Goldsworthy

Poetry ... Ekphrasticly Speaking

The Poetry Posse 2021

Gail Weston Shazor * Albert Carasco * Hülya N. Yılmaz
Jackie Davis Allen * Caroline Nazareno * Eliza Segiet
Alicja Maria Kuberska * Teresa E. Gallion * Joe Paire
Kimberly Burnham * Shareef Abdur – Rasheed
Ashok K. Bhargava * Elizabeth Castillo * Swapna Behera
Tezmin Ition Tsai * William S. Peters, Sr.

The Year of the Poet VIII

December 2021

Featured Global Poets

Orbinda Ganga * Fadairo Tesleem

Anthony Arnold * Iyad Shamasnah

Fredric Edwin Church

Poetry ... Ekphrasticly Speaking

The Poetry Posse 2021

Gail Weston Shazor * Albert Carasco * Hülya N. Yılmaz
Jackie Davis Allen * Caroline Nazareno * Eliza Segiet
Alicja Maria Kuberska * Teresa E. Gallion * Joe Paire
Kimberly Burnham * Shareef Abdur – Rasheed
Ashok K. Bhargava * Elizabeth Castillo * Swapna Behera
Tezmin Ition Tsai * William S. Peters, Sr.

Now Available

www.innerchildpress.com/the-year-of-the-poet

The Year of the Poet IX
January 2022

Featured Global Poets
Ratan Ghosh * Christine Neil-Wright
Andrew Scott * Ashok Kumar

Climate Change : The Ice Cap

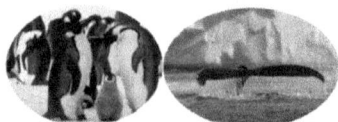

Poetry . . . Ekphrasticly Speaking

The Poetry Posse 2021

Gail Weston Shazor * Albert Carasco * Hülya N. Yılmaz
Jackie Davis Allen * Caroline Nazareno * Eliza Segiet
Alicja Maria Kuberska * Teresa E. Gallion * Joe Paire
Kimberly Burnham * Shareef Abdur – Rasheed
Ashok K. Bhargava * Elizabeth Castillo * Swapna Behera
Tezmin Ition Tsai * William S. Peters, Sr.

The Year of the Poet IX
February 2022

Featured Global Poets
Roza Boyanova * Ramón de Jesús Núñez Duval
Mammad Ismayil * Tarana Turan Rahimli

Climate Change and Mountains

Poetry . . . Ekphrasticly Speaking

The Poetry Posse 2021

Gail Weston Shazor * Albert Carasco * Hülya N. Yılmaz
Jackie Davis Allen * Caroline Nazareno * Eliza Segiet
Alicja Maria Kuberska * Teresa E. Gallion * Joe Paire
Kimberly Burnham * Shareef Abdur – Rasheed
Ashok K. Bhargava * Elizabeth Castillo * Swapna Behera
Tezmin Ition Tsai * William S. Peters, Sr.

The Year of the Poet IX
March 2022

Featured Global Poets
Dimitris P. Kraniotis * Marlene Pasini
Kennedy Ochieng * Swayam Prashant

Climate Change and Space Debris

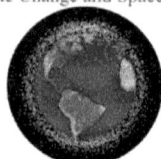

Poetry . . . Ekphrasticly Speaking

The Poetry Posse 2021

Gail Weston Shazor * Albert Carasco * Hülya N. Yılmaz
Jackie Davis Allen * Caroline Nazareno * Eliza Segiet
Alicja Maria Kuberska * Teresa E. Gallion * Joe Paire
Kimberly Burnham * Shareef Abdur – Rasheed
Ashok K. Bhargava * Elizabeth Castillo * Swapna Behera
Tezmin Ition Tsai * William S. Peters, Sr.

The Year of the Poet IX
April 2022

Featured Global Poets
Alonzo Gross * Dr. Debaprasanna Biswas
Monsif Beroual * Carol Aronoff

Climate Change and Oceans

*Celebrating our 100th Edition *

Poetry . . . Ekphrasticly Speaking

The Poetry Posse 2021

Gail Weston Shazor * Albert Carasco * Hülya N. Yılmaz
Jackie Davis Allen * Caroline Nazareno * Eliza Segiet
Alicja Maria Kuberska * Teresa E. Gallion * Joe Paire
Kimberly Burnham * Shareef Abdur – Rasheed
Ashok K. Bhargava * Elizabeth Castillo * Swapna Behera
Tezmin Ition Tsai * William S. Peters, Sr.

Now Available
www.innerchildpress.com/the-year-of-the-poet

The Year of the Poet IX
May 2022

Featured Global Poets
Ndaba Sibanda * Smrutiranjan Mohanty
Ajanta Paul * Monalisa Dash Dwibedy

Climate Change and Birds

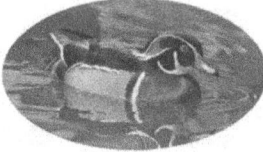

Poetry . . . Ekphrasticly Speaking

The Poetry Posse 2021

Gail Weston Shazor * Albert Carasco * Hülya N. Yılmaz
Jackie Davis Allen * Caroline Nazareno * Eliza Segiet
Alicja Maria Kuberska * Teresa E. Gallion * Joe Paire
Kimberly Burnham * Shareef Abdur – Rasheed
Ashok K. Bhargava * Elizabeth Castillo * Swapna Behera
Tezmin Ition Tsai * William S. Peters, Sr.

The Year of the Poet IX
June 2022

Featured Global Poets
Yuan Changming * Azeezat Okunlola
Tanja Ajtić * Philip Chijioke Abonyi

Climate Change and Trees

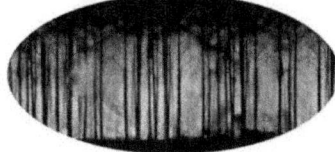

Poetry . . . Ekphrasticly Speaking

The Poetry Posse 2022

Gail Weston Shazor * Albert Carasco * Hülya N. Yılmaz
Jackie Davis Allen * Caroline Nazareno * Eliza Segiet
Alicja Maria Kuberska * Teresa E. Gallion * Joe Paire
Kimberly Burnham * Shareef Abdur – Rasheed
Ashok K. Bhargava * Elizabeth Castillo * Swapna Behera
Tezmin Ition Tsai * William S. Peters, Sr.

The Year of the Poet IX
July 2022

Featured Global Poets
Michelle Joan Barulich * Mili Das
Anna Ferriero * Ujjal Mandal

Climate Change and Animals

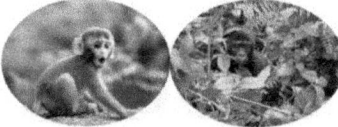

Poetry . . . Ekphrasticly Speaking

The Poetry Posse 2022

Gail Weston Shazor * Albert Carasco * Hülya N. Yılmaz
Jackie Davis Allen * Caroline Nazareno * Eliza Segiet
Alicja Maria Kuberska * Teresa E. Gallion * Joe Paire
Kimberly Burnham * Shareef Abdur – Rasheed
Ashok K. Bhargava * Elizabeth Castillo * Swapna Behera
Tezmin Ition Tsai * William S. Peters, Sr.

The Year of the Poet IX
August 2022

Featured Global Poets
Pankhuri Sinha * Abdulloh Abdumominov
Caroline Turunç * Tali Cohen Shabtai

Climate Change and Agriculture

Poetry . . . Ekphrasticly Speaking

The Poetry Posse 2022

Gail Weston Shazor * Albert Carasco * Hülya N. Yılmaz
Jackie Davis Allen * Caroline Nazareno * Eliza Segiet
Alicja Maria Kuberska * Teresa E. Gallion * Joe Paire
Kimberly Burnham * Shareef Abdur – Rasheed
Ashok K. Bhargava * Elizabeth Castillo * Swapna Behera
Tezmin Ition Tsai * William S. Peters, Sr.

Now Available

www.innerchildpress.com/the-year-of-the-poet

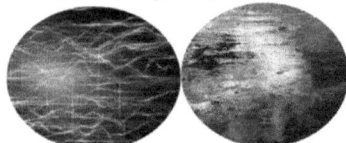
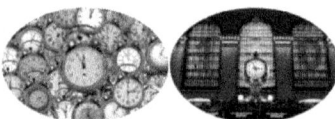
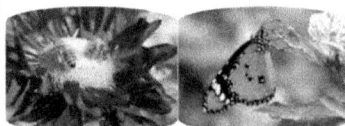

The Year of the Poet X
January 2023

Featured Global Poets

JuNe Barefield * Swayam Prashant
Willow Rose * Shabbirhusein K Jamnagerwalla

Children : Difference Makers

Iqbal Masih

The Poetry Posse 2023

Gail Weston Shazor * Albert Carasco * Hülya N. Yilmaz
Jackie Davis Allen * Caroline Nazareno * Kimberly Burnham
Alicja Maria Kuberska * Teresa E. Gallion * Joe Paire
Michelle Joan Barulich * Shareef Abdur – Rasheed
Ashok K. Bhargava * Elizabeth Castillo * Swapna Behera
Tezmin Ition Tsai * Eliza Segiet * William S. Peters, Sr.

The Year of the Poet X
February 2023

Featured Global Poets

Christena Williams * Hilda Graciela Kraft
Francesco Favetta * Dr. H.C. Louise Hudon

Children : Difference Makers

Ruby Bridges

The Poetry Posse 2023

Gail Weston Shazor * Albert Carasco * Hülya N. Yilmaz
Jackie Davis Allen * Caroline Nazareno * Kimberly Burnham
Alicja Maria Kuberska * Teresa E. Gallion * Joe Paire
Michelle Joan Barulich * Shareef Abdur – Rasheed
Ashok K. Bhargava * Elizabeth Castillo * Swapna Behera
Tezmin Ition Tsai * Eliza Segiet * William S. Peters, Sr.

The Year of the Poet X
March 2023

Featured Global Poets

Clarena Martínez Turizo * Binod Dawadi
Til Kumari Sharma * Petrouchka Alexieva

Children : Difference Makers

Yo Yo Ma

The Poetry Posse 2023

Gail Weston Shazor * Albert Carasco * Hülya N. Yilmaz
Jackie Davis Allen * Caroline Nazareno * Kimberly Burnham
Alicja Maria Kuberska * Teresa E. Gallion * Joe Paire
Michelle Joan Barulich * Shareef Abdur – Rasheed
Ashok K. Bhargava * Elizabeth Castillo * Swapna Behera
Tezmin Ition Tsai * Eliza Segiet * William S. Peters, Sr.

The Year of the Poet X
April 2023

Featured Global Poets

Maxwanette A Poetess * Alonzo Gross
Türkan Ergör * Ibrahim Honjo

Children : Difference Makers

Claudette Colvin

The Poetry Posse 2023

Gail Weston Shazor * Albert Carasco * Hülya N. Yilmaz
Jackie Davis Allen * Caroline Nazareno * Kimberly Burnham
Alicja Maria Kuberska * Teresa E. Gallion * Joe Paire
Michelle Joan Barulich * Shareef Abdur – Rasheed
Ashok K. Bhargava * Elizabeth Castillo * Swapna Behera
Tezmin Ition Tsai * Eliza Segiet * William S. Peters, Sr.

Now Available

www.innerchildpress.com/the-year-of-the-poet

Now Available

and there is much, much more !

visit . . .

www.innerchildpress.com/antho logies-sales-special.php

Also check out our Authors and all the wonderful Books Available at :

www.innerchildpress.com/autho rs-pages

World Healing World Peace
2020

Poets for Humanity

Now Available

www.worldhealingworldpeacepoetry.com

INNER CHILD PRESS

WORLD HEALING
WORLD PEACE
2018

A Poetry Anthology for Humanity

Now Available

www.worldhealingworldpeacepoetry.com

Support

World Healing World Peace

www.worldhealingworldpeacepoetry.com

World Healing
World Peace
2012, 2014, 2016, 2018, 2020, 2022

Now Available

www.worldhealingworldpeacepoetry.com

Inner Child Press International

'building bridges of cultural understanding'

Meet our Cultural Ambassadors

Fahredin Shehu
Director of Cultural

Faleha Hassan
Iraq – USA

Elizabeth E. Castillo
Philippines

Antoinette Coleman
Chicago
Midwest USA

Ananda Nepali
Nepal – Tibet
Northern India

Kimberly Burnham
Pacific Northwest
USA

Alicja Kuberska
Poland
Eastern Europe

Swapna Behera
India
Southeast Asia

Kolade O. Freedom
Nigeria
West Africa

Monsif Beroual
Morocco
Northern Africa

Ashok K. Bhargava
Canada

Tzemin Ition Tsai
Republic of China
Greater China

Alicia M. Ramirez
Mexico
Central America

Christena AV Williams
Jamaica
Caribbean

Louise Hudon
Eastern Canada

Aziz Mountassir
Morocco
Western Africa

Shareef Abdur-Rasheed
Southeastern USA

Laure Charazac
France
Western Europe

Mohammad Ikbal Harb
Lebanon
Middle East

Mohamed Abdel Aziz Sinneis
Egypt
Middle East

Hilary Mainga
Kenya
Eastern Africa

Josephus R. Johnson
Liberia

www.innerchildpress.com

This Anthological Publication
is underwritten solely by

Inner Child Press International

Inner Child Press is a Publishing Company
Founded and Operated by Writers. Our
personal publishing experiences provides
us an intimate understanding of the
sometimes daunting challenges Writers,
New and Seasoned may face in the
Business of Publishing and Marketing
their Creative "Written Work".

For more Information

Inner Child Press International

www.innerchildpress.com

'building bridges of cultural understanding'
202 Wiltree Court, State College, Pennsylvania 16801

www.innerchildpress.com

~ fini ~